Imperfect Vessels

Faith Writings Volume I
Alisa Hope Wagner

Marked Writers Publishing

Imperfect Vessels

Faith Writings Volume I

Imperfect Vessels
Faith Writings Volume I
Copyright @ 2015 by Alisa Hope Wagner
All rights reserved
Marked Writers Publishing
www.alisahopewagner.com

Scriptures taken from multiple translations of the Bible.

Author photo by Monica Lugo
Edits by Faith Newton

ISBN-13: 978-0692415863
ISBN-10: 0692415866
BISAC: Devotional / Christian / Religious/ Nonfiction

Dedication

God, my Creator, my Savior, my Counselor

Daniel, my high school sweetheart and soul mate

Isaac, my firstborn son

Levi, my brown-eyed boy

Karis Ruth, my cherished girl

Christina, my twin and my friend

Cheryl, my spiritual mentor

Forward

This collection of faith writings is book 1 of the *Vessels Series* written over a ten-year span. When a life is given over to God's care, a slow transformation begins to take place. It is difficult to explain this change in a bullet list of conclusions. However, the "ever-increasing" transformation can be experienced in real-life stories. That's what this book represents—a glimpse into the heart of an imperfect person in love with a perfect God.

"And we all, who with unveiled faces contemplate the Lord's glory, are being transformed into his image with ever-increasing glory, which comes from the Lord, who is the Spirit" (2 Corinthians 3.18 NIV).

Vessels Series

Imperfect Vessels
Broken Alabaster Jars
Gathering Empty Pitchers

Imperfect Vessels

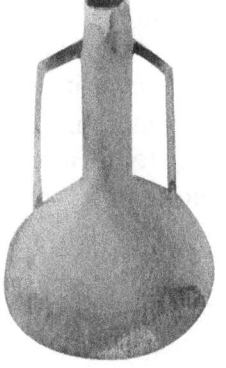

I struggle with a feeling of unworthiness. This feeling is especially crippling when I'm doing things for the Lord. I want to cover up my imperfections, but God won't let me. I wish I could pretend that I was stronger, but I can't. How can I—flawed as I am—do anything right for the kingdom of God? My mistakes are guaranteed. My stumbling is certain. How can I move forward knowing I am not good enough?

I called my spiritual mentor and asked her if I could come by for a visit. We are both busy, but, somehow, God arranged two precious hours for us to sit together at the foot of Jesus' throne. No time existed during those two hours. We were just two souls in the presence of the Spirit of the Holy One. We drew our open hands up to God, grasped pieces of His goodness and exchanged them with each other.

My friend handed me a mug of coffee, and I didn't notice the mug's appearance. I only noticed its feel, and it felt comfortable and perfect. As we chatted, I sipped from the mug, never once looking down at it. She began telling me where she found the mug. She was at a store looking at all the beautiful handmade vessels. While she looked at the perfectly shaped mugs, she saw one that should have been thrown away.

This mug was made too thin and the body of it had collapsed. The maker stretched the body back up, but the damage was already done. The mug was warped with wrinkles and folds, yet the maker still put the mug into the kiln. He added a handle and glazed it and presented it in his store. How could the maker offer an imperfect mug in his shop? Why did he place value on something so flawed?

My friend looked at the mug then looked and me and said, "It's an imperfect vessel, and it's beautiful."

I held the mug protectively in my hands. It might be flawed, but it could still be used. For the first time, I looked at the mug, and I could honestly say that I've never seen a more beautiful vessel in my life. In that moment, I placed a great amount of value on the mug. That imperfect vessel reminded me of myself.

God holds me tightly in His hands, and He places an expensive price tag on my life. I've been weak, and I've crumbled, but He stretched me back up, glazed me with His Spirit and purified me in the fires. Yes, I am flawed, but I am no longer frail. I may have wrinkles and folds, but God thinks I am beautiful. He has fastened me with His handle, and He is ready to use me.

"Do you feel like a lowly worm, Jacob? Don't be afraid. Feel like a fragile insect, Israel? I'll help you. I, God, want to reassure you. The God who buys you back, The Holy One of Israel. I'm transforming you from worm to harrow [a tool used for soil], from insect to iron. As a sharp-toothed harrow you'll smooth out the mountains, turn those tough old hills into loamy soil. You'll open the rough ground to the weather, to the blasts of sun and wind and rain. But you'll be confident and exuberant, expansive in The Holy One of Israel!" (Isaiah 41.14 MSG).

Every fiber in my soul knows that I am nothing in the light of God. If you were to place my spirit next to the Spirit of the Lord, I would completely disappear. It would be like placing a tea candle next to the sun. The more I grow in Christ, the more I comprehend my nothingness without Him.

The story of the immoral woman washing Jesus' feet always bothered me. Jesus forgave the woman of her many sins, and He said, "I tell you, her sins—and they are many—have been forgiven, so she has shown me much love. But a person who is forgiven little shows only little love" (Luke 7.47 NLT).

What I don't think people realize is that we are all immoral. I don't care how the world categorizes and ranks our sins, but compared to the perfection of the Holy God, we are all liars, prostitutes, thieves and murderers. We all have need for great amounts of forgiveness. The only difference between the immoral woman and us is that she comprehended the truth—she is nothing without Him.

The world might label us a sinner or a saint, but it doesn't matter. We are all sinful without the redemption of the cross. We are all the immoral woman at Jesus' feet. The distinction between people who are forgiven much is not their appearance of "many sins"; rather, it is their full understanding and awareness of their "many sins." We all have an outstanding debt of sin that we cannot pay.

All my value and all my self-worth can only come from God. I might be a tea light, but I have the power of the sun around me. I have no significance without my Creator. It's time I let go of finding my own value and start allowing God to place His value on me. I am an imperfect vessel, and God thinks I'm worthy to be used.

God, please help us to shed ourselves of self-confidence, self-worth and self-control and to clothe ourselves with God-confidence, God-worth and God-control. Only then will we truly be beautiful vessels!

Sliding Home

The score was tied in the 9th inning, and we needed one more point to win the championship. My foot rested securely on second base, and I waited for our last hitter to bring me home. (Okay, I might be stretching the truth a little bit. This wasn't the championship and our scores weren't tied, but it does make the story sound better, right?)

I was playing softball for my church college league. I don't really remember the score, but I was alone on second base. I stared at my coach, waiting for her signal. I never watched the batter because that would only slow me down. I watched only my coach; she would tell me what to do.

I heard the "smack" of the ball kissing the bat, and my coach yelled, "Run! Run!" I pushed off second and sprinted toward third. Then my coach's voice screamed, "Go! Go!" When I heard this, I just assumed she meant for me to continue running to home plate. I hadn't made it to third base yet, but I knew I had it. Third base was in the bag. She must be trying to send me home for the score.

When my coach yelled, "Go," I pointed my bullhorns down and charged. I rounded third and kept my eyes on home plate, swinging every limb to propel me forward. Then I heard someone from the dugout yelling, "What is she doing? She's going home!" Of course, I was going home. My coach told me to "Go!"

Over home plate hovered the other team's catcher. She was squatting eye level to me with her glove out. I could tell from the focus in her eyes that she was watching the ball chase me from behind. In a split second, I knew that she was determined to tag me out, but she'd have to jump over my flying body. I was not about to walk off that field quietly.

I dove head-first, sliding across home plate in what felt like slow motion. Dirt billowed around my head, and my body took out anything that was in my way. I heard cheering coming from my dugout, and I knew one of the voices was my coach. I had taken home plate and scored a point.

This is how we are to live as Christians. God is our coach, and when He tells us to "Go," we need to point our bullhorns down and charge. Yes, there will be people saying, "What is she doing?" or "She can't do that!" And there will be people waiting at home plate ready to stop us from fulfilling our destiny. But we can't listen to them. We must trust and obey our God.

God WILL find a way when there is no way. God WILL prove the world wrong. God WILL fulfill His promises to you. So you don't worry about what others think; you just "GO!"

"My sheep hear My voice, and I know them, and they follow Me" (John 10.27 NKJV).

The Handicap

Wikipedia defines Sports Handicapping as follows: "The practice of assigning advantage through scoring compensation or other advantage given to different contestants to equalize the chances of winning."

Keep this definition in mind when you consider Job's question found in Job 9.2: "But how can a mortal be righteous before God?"

There are two ways of achieving such righteousness:
1) Righteousness According to Law
2) Righteousness According to Faith

Ecclesiastes 7.20 (NIV) states: "Indeed, there is no one on earth who is righteous, no one who does what is right and never sins."

Jesus is the only one who can stand in righteousness according to law (2 Corinthians 5.21).

Philippians 3.9 (NIV) states: "and be found in him, not having a righteousness of my own that comes from the law, but that which is through faith in Christ—the righteousness that comes from God and is by faith."

Job (Old Testament) and Paul (New Testament) were both imperfect people. Job had to ask God for forgiveness because he presumed to know the wonders of God (Job 42.5-6). And Paul persecuted Jesus and His disciples (Acts 9.1-5). Both these men had made mistakes, yet they claimed righteousness by faith, and the people hated them for it.

In Job 31.6, Job tells his friends boldly about his righteousness through faith, "Let God weigh me in honest scales and he will know that I am blameless." This upset Job's friends so much that they left him: "So these three men stopped answering Job, because he was righteous in his own eyes" (Job 32.1). The Law had not been given yet, so his righteousness had to be by faith that his actions were pleasing in God's sight.

In Acts 23.1-3 (MSG), Paul proclaims his own righteousness before the High Council: "Paul surveyed the members of the council with a steady gaze, and then said his piece: 'Friends, I've lived with a clear conscience before God all my life, up to this very moment.' That set the Chief Priest Ananias off. He ordered his aides to slap Paul in the face. Paul shot back, 'God will slap you down! What a fake you are! You sit there and judge me by the Law and then break the Law by ordering me slapped around!'"

How can Job and Paul be so bold as to claim their own righteousness when they obviously have not lived perfect lives? They stood strong on a divine handicap that people cannot see. They understood God's grace, and their faith became stronger than their failures.

If we have righteousness through faith in Jesus Christ, why is the world filled with guilt-ridden, insecure Christians? Why are we not claiming the spiritual handicap that is ours through Christ, and determining our victory by the grace God gives us? I believe more Christians would claim their God-given promises and do the impossible for His Kingdom if they truly understood what it meant to be made righteous by faith.

It doesn't matter if the world has video, photos or any other documentation to prove our sin; we have been made righteous through faith in Jesus Christ. We can claim our innocence from the mistakes we made twenty years ago to the mistakes we made today. We can demand a clear conscience because we have a divine handicap that levels the playing field. God packs on the grace, smoothing out the holes of our sin, which gives us an equal chance of winning. Yes, this advantage may upset the people who don't have it, but it's available to all who are willing to receive it.

"By entering through faith into what God has always wanted to do for us—set us right with him, make us fit for him—we have it all together with God because of our Master Jesus. And that's not all: We throw open our doors to God and discover at the same moment that he has already thrown open his door to us. We find ourselves standing where we always hoped we might stand—out in the wide open spaces of God's grace and glory, standing tall and shouting our praise" (Romans 5.1-2 MSG).

Filled

In the Bible, humans are compared to vessels (Roman 9.19-24). We are each beautifully made by the potter, and we all have unique purposes based on our design. However, a vessel's main function is to be filled. God created us to be overflowing with His glory and to pour that glory onto the nations. We cannot be filled with God's glory unless we have the righteousness of Jesus covering us. God is 100% perfect, and He does not commune with anything imperfect. Without Jesus' sacrifice for our sins, we stand flawed and separated from God.

Because of God's grace and our faith, we are miraculously found perfect in God's eyes when we profess our sins, ask for God's forgiveness and receive Jesus in our hearts; and the Holy Spirit can fill us. Even so, God will not force His presence into a Christian's life. We have free will and we can deny the inpouring of the Holy Spirit and keep parts of our heart away from Him. Many Christians refuse God's leading, and they ignorantly believe that they stand-alone. They think that they are neutral and that they direct themselves. What they don't realize is that this is exactly what the enemy wants them to believe.

We never stand-alone. We are vessels; and if we are not filled with the Spirit of God, we may be manipulated by the spirit of the enemy. There are two spiritual waves influencing the world, and we will be pulled by the surge of good or evil. There is no third option. I believe Christians who are saved by grace but not led by the Holy Spirit do more damage to the Kingdom of God than people who are not redeemed. We point our fingers at non-believers and accuse them for living in darkness, yet it is the Christian who has light and chooses to walk in darkness that causes the most confusion.

"…God is light, and in him is no darkness at all. If we say we have fellowship with him while we walk in darkness, we lie and do not practice truth. But if we walk in light, as he is in the light, we have fellowship with one another, and the blood of Jesus his Son cleanses us from all sin" (1 John 1.5-7 NIV).

The enemy wants to sway God's righteous vessels. He plans carefully to knock our lights into sin. He wants to prove that he is strong, so he leads us to believe that our vessels can remain empty. Secretly, though, the enemy begins to fill us with his ugliness; and before we know it, we are lost in a black hole of compromise and sin. The world watches us fall, while mocking our faith and our God.

I pray every day for God to fill me with His Spirit. I know I am a vessel, and I know the enemy would like nothing better than to fill me with his influences. This knowledge gives me a holy fear. I am not blind to the enemy's schemes. I know that if I'm not yoked to Jesus that I will be yoked by another who wants to deceive, hurt and destroy me. The world can offer me all its beautifully painted delicacies of sin, but I'm not falling for it. I will stand firm in the promises of God.

"Set a guard, O LORD, over my mouth; keep watch over the door of my lips! Do not let my heart incline to any evil, to busy myself with wicked deeds in company with men who work iniquity, and let me not eat of their delicacies!" (Psalm 141.3-4 NIV).

God is faithful. As Christians, our souls are secure in heaven because of Jesus' righteousness covering us. But God also gives us free will. We must choose to yoke ourselves with Jesus every day (Matthew 11.29). Only then can we be guided into God's best for our lives. Otherwise, we become puppets for the father of all lies (John 8.44). There is a purpose for our existence on this earth, and we need to "be wise as serpents and innocent as doves" (Matthew 10.16). Only then can we achieve our predetermined victories in Christ.

Wrestling with God

I wrestle with God a lot. Like Jacob, God leads me to a place of transition, and the core of who I am is exposed. God points out a deep-rooted sin, and He waits on me to make a choice: Will I allow Him to uproot the ugliness or will I run and hide from His hand? If I let God do spiritual surgery on my heart, I will have spiritual health to carry the weight of His blessings. If I run and hide from this divine appointment, I will be filled with my own ugliness and unable to bear His fullness in my life.

Out of obedience, Jacob moved forward with God until he was stuck in a place of transition. He couldn't run back to Laban (his father-in-law), yet he feared going forward to Esau (his brother). Jacob's deceitful past was catching up to him, and he ran out of hiding places. With nowhere to turn, he had to confront the facts—he was a deceiver (Genesis 32).

God had been blessing Jacob even though he had this character flaw. God provided Jacob with children, servants, riches, authority, etc. However, God wanted to bless Jacob at a new level, but Jacob needed some excess baggage cut off. Jacob couldn't move forward into God's abundance because he was tied down by his sin.

Finally, Jacob confronted God face to face and had an all-out wrestling match. The interesting thing about wrestling with God is that God never moves or changes. God is perfect and unchanging. If we decide to take Him on, we will be the ones who move and change.

When we wrestle with God, we become meek. Meekness means that we allow God complete control over our lives, so that we can have the fullness of His glory, power and strength displayed through us. If you want the power of God, wrestle with Him whenever He calls you into the ring. Let God be the Divine Director of your life, and He will use you to shine His glory.

I used to try to avoid wrestling with God. I thought that if I could just pray hard enough and keep my ears focused on the Holy Spirit, that I would be good enough to bypass this painful encounter with Him. I thought I could change myself without feeling the pruning of His hand.

I've learned to embrace it! I want to be blessed by God; and if I have to wrestle with Him and allow my sinful nature to be cut, then so be it. I want His blessings more than I want a painless, carefree life.

How do you know that God is inviting you to a wrestling match? Just remember **M E E K.**

Moving: You feel a movement of God and obediently follow His lead.

Exposing: You feel God revealing an area of selfishness in your life, and you can't move forward but you won't retreat.

Extracting: You feel God cutting away hidden sin and endure for the promised blessings.

Kneeling: You feel changed in Christ and are more aware of His majesty and glory.

I don't know about you, but I want to wrestle with God. Do not feel guilty when you go through this process. It is not a sign of your lack of faith. It is a sign that you hunger for Him more than you hunger for comfortable and easy. So get into the ring! I promise that you will lose, but you will gain His blessings!

"Then the man said, 'Let me go, for it is daybreak.' But Jacob replied, 'I will not let you go unless you bless me'" (Genesis 32.26 NIV).

Your Part in the Wall

I was reading in my one year Bible about the remnant rebuilding the wall after they returned to Jerusalem. Two very different prophets were called by God to oversee the construction of the wall and to help reestablish the nation. So much insight can be gleaned from this story, but I'm excited about what God made personal to me (Nehemiah 1-7).

After reading Ezra's and Nehemiah's points-of-view, I felt God ask me, "Which one do you think you are?" I excitedly told God, "Nehemiah!" In my mind's eye, I could see God turn His head toward me, raise His eyebrow and say, "Really?" I read back through the details from both prophets, and I knew I was more like Ezra.

When I was twenty-five years old, I taught college composition. This was the hardest step of obedience I had taken up to that point. For a solid year, I lived on the opposite side of my comfort zone. The emotional, spiritual and physical pressure I felt squashed my appetite, and I became the thinnest I've ever been in my adult life. Although I was a good teacher and the students learned a lot and enjoyed my class, I was anxious all of the time.

I didn't like being in front of a class. I didn't like everyone looking at me for direction and answers. I didn't like having to talk, talk, talk all the time. I was definitely no Nehemiah. I would have preferred to sit among the students, read my books and lead by example. God knew this time would stretch me, so, thankfully, He didn't ask me to teach college for long. He gave me a full year to rest before He put me through another stretching situation (my first baby).

The interesting thing is that if God were to ask me this question several years ago, I would have insisted on the wrong answer. I get so enamored by the action and risk of Nehemiah that I forget about the heart and strength of Ezra. Both these prophets were necessary to the completion of the wall. They both brought God's vision to fruition by each doing his different, yet equal part.

I think the reason that many Christians feel jealous, angry or confused about what other Christians are achieving is because they don't know what they're supposed to be doing. It is hard to know who we are in Christ if we don't know who we are.

I used to feel guilty about self-evaluation, like it was egocentric. But God reprimanded me. He said that I needed to have a healthy understanding of my design, my desires and my destiny. We all must find our wall (purpose), that grows His temple (church) and plant our house (life) in the middle of it.

When we find our niche in God's Kingdom here on earth, we will find ourselves in Holy Ease. This doesn't mean everything will be easy or smooth, but our passion should align with our purpose. Nehemiah and Ezra did a lot of work against all odds and showed great amounts of discipline, and they were able to achieve the impossible.

Together they built the wall in 52 days and established God's people on His truth. God divided His vision, and everyone did his and her part. How much could the church accomplish today if Christians would discover their part and do it wholeheartedly?

Have you asked God to give you a healthy understanding of who you are in Him? If you saw some of your personality reflecting from a Bible character, would you recognize yourself? How do you think knowing your design will help you achieve your destiny?

"Because of the privilege and authority God has given me, I give each of you this warning: Don't think you are better than you really are. Be honest in your evaluation of yourselves, measuring yourselves by the faith God has given us. Just as our bodies have many parts and each part has a special function, so it is with Christ's body. We are many parts of one body, and we all belong to each other" (Romans 12.3-5 NIV).

Empty Carton

Have you ever watched a character in a milk commercial drink from a carton? The character lifts the milk to his lips, and the carton appears virtually weightless. After the character takes his drink, you wait for the swallow, but it never comes. The character offers an indulgent smile, yet there is not a drop of milk on his lips. Commercials try to creatively make the carton appear full, yet there is nothing in it. The effort used to put on this charade begs the question, "Why not just drink from a carton that is full?"

The sad truth is that we Christians do the same thing in our walks of faith. We tend to embrace the performance of our faith rather than embrace the Maker of our faith. We are diligent about managing our ministries, serving others and gaining biblical knowledge, yet we slack on knowing our God more intimately. We don't do it on purpose. Our intentions are never to take our focus off of God and place it on our performance for God, but we do. We are so busy serving Him that we don't have time to spend with Him. We fall into performance-based spirituality, and our relationship with God takes a back seat.

Performance-based spirituality is one of the main plugs stopping the flow of the Holy Spirit. We forget that God is infinitely creative and has a plethora of resources at His disposal. We can never assume that we know how our steps of obedience are going to play out: "A person's steps are directed by the LORD. How then can anyone understand their own way?" (Proverbs 20.24 NIV). Yet, without consulting God, we get a spiritual performance (ministry, service, tradition, etc.) in our mind, and we work hard to achieve it—even if it costs us our time with God.

In this culture today we are very busy, and we complain to God that there isn't enough time to spend with Him. However, our time is God's number one desire. If we don't give God our time, how are we expected to cultivate a relationship with Him? God would never ask us to serve Him in a way that prevented us from spending time with Him.

In the book of Mark, a religious leader asked Jesus which commandment was the most important, and Jesus replied, "Love the Lord your God with all your heart and with all your soul and with all your mind and with all your strength" (12.30 NIV). If loving God is the highest commandment, why would God put us in a circumstance that conflicts with spending time with Him?

Today we have so many choices, which force us to daily make hundreds of decisions. What should we watch, read, eat and wear? What ministry should we support? What online social network should we join? What ideology (way of thinking) should we commit to? What social cause should we embrace? What life purpose should we focus on?

If we are not carefully walking in the Spirit, we're going to be overwhelmed with choices and begin to second-guess ourselves. We will become bogged down in a swamp of choice, and our purpose of reaching our full potential in Christ will be jeopardized.

There are thousands of great ministries, media venues, compassion campaigns and people doing a good work for God's kingdom. However, if our spiritual walks are performance-based, we may find ourselves lost in a market full of good work vendors and no guide to lead us in the right direction. These vendors line our path and call out our names, trying to persuade us that their good work is an absolute must for our walk of faith.

There is nothing wrong with these good works, but the Holy Spirit has to daily show us which ones we should carry and which ones we should let go. If we are not allowing the Holy Spirit to direct us, we'll carry the same good works forever and pile on more until our views become blocked and our arms become heavy.

Moreover, if all of our time and energy is spent on performance-based spirituality and not on God, those good works become idols. God specifically says that He hates it when we cling to idols instead of trusting Him (Psalm 31.6). When we desire a relationship with God and strive to know Him more, our good works will be an outflow of the Holy Spirit working in us.

We won't have to worry about doing the wrong good works or doing too many good works because God promises that if we put Him first, He'll take care of everything: "But seek first his kingdom and his righteousness, and all these things will be given to you as well" (Matthew 6.33 NIV). Our purpose in life is to have an intimate relationship with our Creator; everything else is merely icing on the cake!

If you are feeling overwhelmed and stretched thin, take a few moments to have an honest discourse with God. Ask Him if there are any areas of your life that you have been "drinking from an empty carton." He will show you. Give those areas over to God and let go of your idea of what your spiritual walk should look like.

Choose to put knowing God intimately as your highest priority, and He will free you from performance-based spirituality. Make sure that in everything you do that the carton is filled with God's Spirit. In this way, you will ensure that you don't waste your time and energy on empty performances that leave you feeling unfulfilled, tired and malnourished.

Don't Claim Ownership

The enemy hands out temptations every chance he gets. He and his cohorts save stacks and stacks of them. They stand on street corners and force them into the hands of anyone who walks by. Sometime the temptations are carefully planned, but many times they're just thrown out in droves in hopes that they'll eventually be picked up.

The sad thing is that many Christians feel obliged to take them. They see the temptation staring them in the face and have no clue what to do with it, so they quickly grab it and tuck it away in their hearts before anyone sees. They feel ashamed that such a temptation had ever been offered to them, like it's their fault the enemy wants to see them fall. I've done this so many times. I'm embarrassed by a temptation that's being handed to me, so I quickly take it and hide it inside. I feel that if I were somehow a better person or if I were closer to God that the enemy wouldn't have access. Though I usually never do anything with the temptation, I still feel guilty. That guilt trips me up and distracts me from the beautiful things God is doing in my life.

I'm sure the enemy hopes that the temptation will linger and grow roots, but he's satisfied with our guilty feelings. If we're constantly feeling guilty, we're not going to be very confident Christians. And if we're not confident Christians, it will be hard to be a Christ-like example to this world.

I finally read something that was so simple and obvious, but I just never applied it to my life: "Then Jesus was led by the Spirit into the desert to be tempted by the devil" (Matthew 4.1 NIV). The perfect Son of God was tempted, and I'm going to go out on a limb and suggest that Satan attacked Jesus with EVERYTHING in his arsenal. So whatever small or outrageous temptation we are given, Jesus was probably given it too. And please note that the "Spirit" led Jesus into the desert to be tempted. That's an entirely different topic, but the Bible does say that God tests the hearts of His children: "The refining pot is for silver and the furnace for gold, but the Lord tests the hearts" (Proverbs 17.3 NKJV).

I bet Jesus was tempted a lot—much more than what is documented in the Bible. Satan pumps up his attacks against anyone who is serving the Kingdom of God, and Jesus is the supreme Servant. But Jesus never took ownership of those temptations. He rebuked them, and He never felt guilt over them. How could He? He is the perfect Son of God. Jesus has no reason to feel guilt.

Now when I walk down the street and those temptations are being thrust at me left and right, I'm going to give them to God. They have no power over me. In fact, God promises to never let us face temptation that we are unable to claim victory over (1 Corinthians 10.13). I will also search my heart for temptations that I've surrounded with guilt and tucked away. I'm going to expose them to God, so they will no longer have any control over my life. God gives me a choice over what I claim ownership. Forget the temptations and guilt! I'll take more blessings and peace!

"This day I call the heavens and the earth as witnesses against you that I have set before you life and death, blessings and curses. Now choose life, so that you and your children may live" (Deuteronomy 30.19 NIV).

The 300 Club

"But the Lord said to Gideon, 'There are still too many men. Take them down to the water, and I will thin them out for you there. If I say, 'This one shall go with you,' he shall go; but if I say, 'This one shall not go with you,' he shall not go'" (Judges 7.4 NIV).

My husband is intrigued by the story of God forming Gideon's army to fight against the Midianites. We discuss this story together because we crave to be part of the 300 men God uses to show His glory. We all know that God slims down the army of 32,000 so He can ensure that the victory is obviously His alone. However, why does God choose to use those particular men? What is different about them that they are granted the honor of fighting? How can Christians today ensure that we are part of the infamous 300 Club?

Finally, after much conversation and study, my husband and I came up with three characteristics that separate these men from the crowd. I believe every single man among the 32,000 had an opportunity to serve God, but each chose to bow out of God's plan by A) his lack of trust in God, B) his lack of hunger for God and C) his lack of obedience to God. God wants all of His children to share in His glory, but He gives us free will to choose. Whether or not we are willing to be a part of God's amazing adventure is up to us.

God first whittles down the army by allowing those who were afraid to leave the fight and go home. Twenty-two thousand men walk out on the amazing demonstration that God is about to perform. I believe that this is the number one reason today Christians do not fulfill their destiny – they are afraid. This fear shows a lack of trust in God, and this lack stops the blessings of God. Psalm 84.12 (NIV) reads, "O LORD Almighty, blessed is the man who trusts in you." The men who show courage trust that God is about to do something spectacular, and they know that they will share in the bounty.

Only 10,000 men are left after the doubtful leave. These are the men who trust in God and want to do His will, but the question is "Do they thirst for God?" God tells Gideon to have all the men go down to the water to take a drink. Although the Bible doesn't specify, I believe not all 10,000 men make the trek down to the water. I'm sure many of the men did not feel thirsty, so they decide to stay behind on dry land. Jesus said in Matthew 5.6 (NIV), "Blessed are those who hunger and thirst for righteousness, for they will be filled." The men who thirst for God have a desire to do His will, but the men who do not desire Him will stay behind.

Finally, at the water source, God separates the men one more time. Not only must we trust God and thirst for Him, we have to be obedient to His nontraditional and sometimes crazy will. Out of all the men who drank water, only 300 of them lapped it up like a dog, and those are the men God could use. Although the entire image of lapping water has many implications, I'm fascinated that God chose the men who go against the norm, who are different.

What I've learned about God is that He is not predictable, and He doesn't do things the way the world does. Jesus is the prime example. The world expected a King, but God gave them a Carpenter. Job declares in Job 37.5 (NIV), "God's voice thunders in marvelous ways; he does great things beyond our understanding." God does things differently, and if we crave to do His will, we can't worry about what others are doing. Our obedience to God will cause us to stand out in mainstream culture.

God employed those 300 men to defeat the Midianites in a way that would not be documented in any wartime strategy manual. In fact, if each man did not trust God, thirst for Him and obey Him, the army would never have been able to pull off a victory—everything centered on God's ability and the men's compliance.

There was no room for fear, selfishness or disobedience. Each man had to be crazy in love with God and willing to execute His bizarre plan. My desire for all Christians is that we make it into God's 300 Club. We don't have to be smart, popular or perfect; we just have to want God more than anything.

The Accuser

"Then I heard a loud voice in heaven say: 'Now have come the salvation and the power and the kingdom of our God, and the authority of his Christ. For the accuser of our brothers, who accuses them before our God day and night, has been hurled down'" (Revelation 12.10 NIV).

I recently read this verse in Revelation, and I received a better understanding of what I'm up against when trying to live a sold-out life for Christ. I have an enemy who accuses me day in and day out. And he is very good at what he does. I've only been on this earth for a short time; the accuser has been on this earth since time began. He has practiced his schemes on every generation since Adam and Eve, so I am no surprise to him. The accuser looks at me and thinks, "Piece of cake."

There is no way that I will be able to claim victory over this accuser on my own. I might as well admit defeat because I am out-smarted and out-matched. Thankfully, God knows that I would lose in my own strength, so He tells me to die to my weak self and live in the power that He has given me (Luke 9.23-24).

Dying to self is very hard at first, but it gets easier when we begin to see first-hand what God can accomplish in our lives when our selfish dictatorships are out of the way. Once I learned to forgo my plans and cling to God's, I discovered a life that was worthy to be lived—a life that produced a harvest for God's Kingdom.

When we let go of our limited understanding, we gain the mind of Christ (1 Corinthians 2.16). The enemy may out-smart us, but Jesus Christ out-smarts him. Jesus proved this on the cross when He defeated death. Moreover, Christ renews our mind, and we leave the predictable patterns of the world that the enemy is well versed in. The enemy knows how to make us fall, but the renewing of our minds in Christ will keep the enemy guessing (Romans 12.2).

Also, when we realize that we are weaker than our enemy, we will rightly give control over to the Holy Spirit. God's Spirit in us is like having a perfect guide, perfect leader, perfect parent and perfect compass in our lives. We are out-matched by ourselves, but the Holy Spirit greatly tips the scales in our favor (John 14.26). Although the enemy may be accusing us, God's Spirit is constantly interceding for us. I can only imagine that the accuser's accusations are petty compared to the amazing things God's Spirit says about us (Romans 8.27).

But who are we listening to? Are we listening and believing in the enemy's accusations or are we listening and believing in God's truth? I once believed that it was normal to allow my mind to accuse myself, but I discovered that I was doing the enemy's will. I want to do the will of God. I want to proclaim my victory and my value according to God's truth established for me. What is God's truth? He loves me. He loves you. He loves us enough to die for our sins so that we can commune with a holy God through the righteousness we gain by faith in Jesus Christ (1 John 4.10) and (Romans 5.17).

I think if we fully understood God's love for us, we would instantly embrace His will for our lives. He has such an amazing plan for all of us—a plan that we could never comprehend or fulfill without Him (1 Corinthians 2.9). I want to stop listening and believing in the enemy, so I can keep my ears and eyes focused on how God wants to display His glory through my life. I don't know about you, but I'm ready to listen to what God says about me.

"With this in mind, we constantly pray for you, that our God may count you worthy of his calling, and that by his power he may fulfill every good purpose of yours and every act prompted by your faith. We pray this so that the name of our Lord Jesus may be glorified in you, and you in him, according to the grace of our God and the Lord Jesus Christ" (2 Thessalonians 1.11-12 NIV).

Peaceful Swords

Our world is a colony, established by God to emulate His Divine Kingdom (heaven) here on earth. The Holy Spirit is our Colonial Ambassador, living amongst us, guiding and teaching us in the ways of our perfect King. The Holy Spirit's job is to saturate our world with Kingdom-influence so that God's children will become like their Father. The Holy Spirit is able to lead each person whose sins have been atoned by the sacrifice of Jesus Christ on the cross.

Jesus is our Prince of Peace because He is our only link to the King's abundant peace (Isaiah 9.6). God is Holy and faithfully undivided; He is the source of all peace. We cannot fully understand His divine peace until we're on the other side of eternity (Philippians 4.7). Christians have this Source of Peace inside each of us—a gift promised by the resurrected Jesus (John 14.26).

Sin penetrated our special colony, so our environment has become corrupt, our bodies decay and people hurt each other. We live in a world of unrest and conflict. We capture moments of peace only to have them swept away by the tide of disorder. We grope onto pitiful worldly understandings, desperately seeking illusions of peace. But peace—pure and endless—can be found generously within the Spirit God breathed into each of us.

Be assured, though, Christians go against the grain of world's culture, and we will cause turmoil because of the name of Jesus Christ. Jesus says, "Do not suppose that I have come to bring peace to the earth. I did not come to bring peace, but a sword" (Matthew 10.34 NIV). Christians will not agree with much of the world-view, and this will create division. We will be spotlighted as Bible-thumping troublemakers. The colony has declared independence from our holy and perfect King and the heaven we were meant to represent. Indeed, Christian influence will disrupt the world's agenda if we are to stay sanctified and set apart (1 Thessalonians 4.3).

However, Jesus also tells us to pursue harmony. He says, "….Have salt in yourselves, and be at peace with each other" (Mark 9.50 NIV). As a church, we need to swallow our pride to keep the peace and put the unity of the Body of Christ above our own desires (Colossians 3.15). As Christians, we should serve others and eliminate our self-entitlement and our perceived rights. Our goal should be to strengthen the Church, so we can be used by the Holy Spirit to spread His Kingdom-influence.

But how do we know when we should pursue peace or division? When should our sanctified lives sever or unite? When should we be swords or peacemakers?

Swords: We cut away unholy influences with truth to keep the Church sanctified.

Peacemakers: We deny our self-will to promote peace in the Church.

The Holy Spirit lets us know when to separate the Body of Christ from the world's influence and when to lay down our rights for the sake of church harmony. This is every Christian's balancing act, and we must be completely submitted to the Holy Spirit if we want to be the peaceful sword that God has called us to be. God's Truth will build the church and offend the world, and Christians are called to do both. But even as we slice off sin for church sanctification or cut off our personal rights for church harmony, we still have the peace of God in our spirits—and that's how we become Peaceful Swords!

Moving Mountains

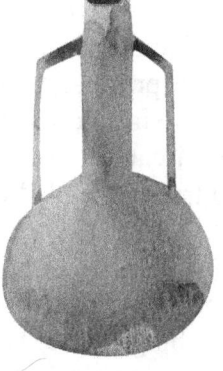

"Truly I tell you, if anyone says to this mountain, 'Go, throw yourself into the sea,' and does not doubt in their heart but believes that what they say will happen, it will be done for them'" (Mark 11.23 NIV).

Like any great writer or orator, Jesus chose His words carefully. He paints an awesome picture of faith in the above promise, but I think we miss so much when we don't explore why Jesus would choose the metaphor "mountain." If a mountain were to fall into the sea, it would be a natural disaster of monstrous proportions, destroying everything in its wake.

Since I don't think that Jesus really wanted Christians calling mountains into the sea, I have to believe that He chose this word for a specific reason. As we dig for understanding in His Word, so much treasure comes up that it's hard to take it all in. The symbol of a mountain is used many times in the Old and New Testament. God's glory appears on the mountain and people experience supernatural phenomena; but I've noticed that most of the time, the people have to climb up the mountain to be a part of what God is doing.

Abraham climbed a mountain to sacrifice Isaac (Genesis 22.2). Moses saw a burning bush (Exodus 3.1), received God's laws (Exodus 24.12), and saw God Himself (Exodus 33.21-22) on a mountain. Elijah heard the voice of God on a mountain (1 Kings 19.11). Isaiah and Micah both promise that the Lord's Temple will be established on a mountain and God's people will make their way to it (Isaiah 2.1-5) (Micah 4.1-5). Jesus led Peter, James and John up a mountain and transfigured (Matthew 17.1-3).

So many times, we want God to move our mountain, but from reading Scripture, I think God wants us to climb it first. I quickly researched the process of climbing a mountain, and it is not easy. Mount Everest is the highest mountain in the world. In order to ascend it, you must sacrifice a lot of money and time, find guides who are knowledgeable and go through a strenuous and lengthy acclimation process.

Mount Everest is 8,848 meters above sea level, and anything above 8,000 meters is called the "death zone," because one cannot survive for more than two or three days in it. Complete oxygen saturation in the body is impossible, even when taking three times as many breaths. Most people bring portable oxygen to ease the stress on the body. The wind, weather, freezing temperature and slick ice all add to the implausibility of reaching the top.

When climbers start out, they must move slowly so that their bodies can assimilate to the ascension. At sea level our bodies have 98% - 99% oxygen saturation. At the base camp of Mount Everest (5,380 meters) the oxygen saturation is already at around 85% and there is still a mountain left to climb! In order to acclimate to the altitude, climbers will "climb high, sleep low." I find this interesting because it sounds like wasted time, but the climbers push their bodies during the day and retreat to lower altitudes during the night to help their bodies get used to the height.

When we imagine mountains in our spiritual lives, we think of Exodus 15.17 (NLT): "You will bring them in and plant them on the mountain of your inheritance—the place, LORD, you made for your dwelling, the sanctuary, Lord, your hands established." God plants our inheritance or His promises on the mountaintops. Often times we beg God to fulfill His promises to us; yet if He did, we would surely die. We will NEVER get acclimated to His anointing for our lives if we don't climb up the mountain—the climb is what prepares us for the summit!

Some people wonder why God would put His promises on mountaintops if mountains are so difficult to climb. Why wouldn't He make it easier on us and simply lay our promises at our feet? The one human condition that robs us of serving God is serving self. If the promises were strewn at our feet, we would stay in our selfish state. Instead, God plants His promises on His mountain at His feet (Psalm 132.7-8), so we can have an encounter with Him. This earth, our souls and life in general were created to know Him; because in forming a personal relationship with our Creator, we find our purpose, our joy and our true love.

"How beautiful on the mountains are the feet of those who bring good news, who proclaim peace, who bring good tidings, who proclaim salvation, who say to Zion, 'Your God reigns!'" (Isaiah 52.7 NIV).

When we finally reach the mountaintop, our own feet become beautiful because we have finally discovered the meaning of our existence. We are to proclaim God's peace and salvation to the world. We are to use His promises for our lives to tell the world about Christ—any other reason would be idolatrous. We are to yell from the mountaintops that God created us because of His glory, Jesus sacrificed Himself for our sins so we can commune with a perfect God, and the Holy Spirit lives in each of us, guiding us through the mountains and valleys of our lives.

The climb to the top changes us. We sacrifice all we have and are then filled with God's glory because now our emptied selves have room for Him. And when we finally make it to the pinnacle, our faith causes the mountain to fall into the sea! Jesus gives us a beautiful promise: the highest point of that mountain—a place where we can't survive on our own—supernaturally becomes sea level. We can now function at 99% oxygen saturation on a mountaintop that we could never have survived before we started our journey up.

But don't get too comfortable on that sea-level mountain for long. God will place another mountain in your horizon. Don't worry, though, I'm sure He'll let you rest before He expects you to gather your climbing gear. And just remember, "climb high, sleep low." God will give you rest on the mountain, and He'll never push you beyond what you are capable of doing. The climb may take years, but Jesus never mentioned a timetable when He promised the mountain would be moved.

Take a good look at the mountaintop before you start your ascension; you won't be able to see it until you make it to the "death zone," and God supernaturally throws the summit into sea level for you. You'll have to press forward by faith, knowing that God gave you a vision of the mountaintop and planted your inheritance at His feet.

* Mountain research from Team Everest 03 and Wikipedia.

Righteous Hunger

"For I tell you that unless your righteousness surpasses that of the Pharisees and the teachers of the law, you will certainly not enter the kingdom of heaven" (Matthew 5.20 NIV).

Jesus just started His ministry. He chose His disciples and began to heal the afflicted. He brought His disciples to the top of the mountain and told them that they needed to be more righteous than the Pharisees. I'm sure these fishermen were pretty overwhelmed. They just began their ministry with Jesus, and already He expected too much from these average men. How could they be more righteous than the religious leaders?

The disciples probably became more bewildered when later on in the Book of Matthew, Jesus told them to be on their guard against the Pharisees' influence (16.6) and when He called the religious leaders whitewashed tombs (23.27). Jesus overlooked all kinds of sin with His grace, but the religious leaders were the main source of His righteous anger because of their hypocrisy (Matthew 23.1-8). Jesus went so far as to give the religious leaders Seven Woes (Matthew 23.13-37).

The highest level of righteousness was based on the Laws of Moses made on Mount Sinai. The laws were a standard for a Hebrew nation thousands of years ago in love with their God—the laws were supposed to be an outward show of an inward heart. However, as time passed the rigorous laws became an outward show of self-righteousness, instead of God-righteousness. Soon the heart for God was replaced by hypocrisy and pretense, which left the masses confused and spiritually lost.

The understanding of righteousness becomes the primary internal conflict of the New Testament. The standard of righteousness was set by religious leaders, but Jesus made it clear that this standard was not His divine standard. The word righteousness that is found in Matthew 6.33 and Matthew 5.6 is the Greek word, dikaiosynē, which means "condition acceptable to God" or "a state approved of God." The religious leaders were deceived. Their righteousness was based on the acceptance and approval of people, not God.

So how can we gain acceptance and approval from God?

"And be found in him, not having a righteousness of my own that comes from the law, but that which is through faith in Christ—the righteousness that comes from God on the basis of faith" (Philippians 3.9 NIV).

No matter how good we think we are, we will never gain right-standing with God on our own. We are covered with Jesus' righteousness when we accept His sacrifice by faith. Jesus is God in the flesh who freely took our sins on the cross over two thousand years ago, so we might have right-standing with God and live with Him for eternity. But our righteousness doesn't end there.

If all we had to do was gain Jesus' righteousness by faith, there would be no reason to stay on this earth. God not only wants to cover us with His righteousness; He wants to fill us with His righteousness. Once we are saved, God places His Spirit inside of us, in order to transform us into His likeness: "And we all, who with unveiled faces contemplate the Lord's glory, are being transformed into his image with ever-increasing glory, which comes from the Lord, who is the Spirit" (2 Corinthians 3.18 NIV).

God allows us to stay in this broken world, so that we may become like Him. I believe that many Christians—either out of fear or ignorance—stay clear of spiritual transformation. They sit content in their wedding clothes but never bother to get to know their King (Parable of the Wedding Banquet: Matthew 22.1-14). I was once such a Christian. I allowed myself to be too busy, too distracted and too self-focused to get to know my Creator. He had to break me, so He could get my attention. And I'm glad He did.

Our righteousness starts out as a spiritual seed, but that seed should manifest itself into physical fruits. People should see a difference in us. They should notice that we have more "love, joy, peace, patience, kindness, goodness, faithfulness, gentleness, and self-control" (Galatians 5.22-23 NLT). People should see us walking on Paths of Righteousness (Psalm 23). We should be gaining the Mind of Christ (1 Corinthians 2.16) and be filled with the Power of the Holy Spirit (Acts 1.8). However, this transformation will not happen overnight nor without sacrifice (Philippians 3.8).

But how do we start this transformation journey?

We seek it: "But seek first his kingdom and his righteousness, and all these things will be given to you as well" (Matthew 6.33 NIV).

We hunger for it: "Blessed are those who hunger and thirst for righteousness, for they will be filled" (Matthew 5.6 NIV).

"We live in order that our souls may grow. The development of the soul is the purpose of our existence." - John G. Lake

Watercolor Faith

My spiritual mentor paints with watercolors. She has taught beginning courses in that medium, and she honored me with one of her originals. Painting with watercolors, she explained, is an interesting process. The artist sketches an outline that presents the path, but the diluted colors usually add their own forms and shapes along the way. The water in the color cannot be fully controlled, which can cause frustration if the artist is not willing to "go with the flow." It takes faith to trust that the water knows what it's doing.

Another difficult aspect of using watercolor is that you can't make changes. Once the color hits the page, there is no turning back. You can't paint over it because the paint is too translucent to hide what's beneath; and you can't scrape it off because the paint binds with the paper. All you can do is learn to anticipate the movement of the water. The more an artist study's the flow of water, the better she will become at working with it. The end result is beautiful. The sketches underneath are fixed, but the colors around the lines take on their own life. The entire painting is a masterpiece of skill, imagination and faith.

When I placed my friend's painting only inches from my face, I couldn't see the distinction between each object. All the colors blended into each other, and I couldn't tell what I was looking at. However, when I stepped several feet away from the painting, I could see the objects in detail. How could that be? My friend explained that your mind completes the shapes by drawing conclusions on what it sees. I saw sunglasses on a man's face and a hat on his head from far away, but up close it just looked like smudges of translucent paint. I gained a better perspective from a distance.

My walk with God is a lot like painting with watercolors. I sketch out my plans, but God's movement never seems to stay in the lines. When I look real close at what He's doing in my life, I become confused and frustrated. His will doesn't seem to make sense to me, and I don't understand how it's all going to work out. Also, I make mistakes, and I know they are erased in His eyes, but they seem to always be there on my painting—never fully covered over or scraped off. They appear so ugly to me!

But God finally showed me through my friend that I'm looking too closely. I need to take a few steps back and look at my life from His perspective. He is the Master Painter, and He knows exactly what He's doing. He doesn't take over. He allows my imagination and passion to decide the subject, but His Spirit does flow through the pages of my life.

God doesn't cover up my sketches or scrape off my mistakes; instead, He shows off by incorporating my limited talent and redeemed sin into His perfect design. He works with each of us to make a one-of-the-kind masterpiece; and we have faith that our paintings will be hanging on the walls of His temple, telling the story of His glory in our lives.

"And we know that in all things God works for the good of those who love him, who have been called according to his purpose" (Romans 8.28 NIV).

A Father's Glory

Why were humans created clothed in flesh? The angels weren't. They were born directly into the glory and wonders of God. The flesh does force us to build and use our faith, but what is so important about faith? I believe faith gives us the Father. Let me explain.

Billy Graham in his book, *Angels*, writes that "God is not called 'Father' by the holy angels because, not having sinned, they need not be redeemed." I wondered, "Why can't the angels call God *Father*? What about the flesh and our faith makes the difference?"

The flesh covers the glory of God. Yes, we can see manifestations of it here on this earth; however, they are nothing compared to what the angels see. When I read the descriptions of God's glory that is experienced by the angels, I know that I have seen very little of it. I trust that His glory is amazing, but I must have faith. I have not seen heaven yet.

Why is it so important that we be shielded from the fulness of God's glory? What about knowing this glory first as the angels did caused them to lose the ability to experience God as a Father?

Think of the most famous person you know. Now imagine meeting him or her. Would you be nervous? Would you be star-struck? Would you cry tears? Would you have a dramatic emotional response even though you don't know him or her personally? Now imagine compounding that emotion and awe by infinity, and you might come close to the reaction you will have when you meet God and His glory.

No matter how your relationship evolves with that famous person, your initial reaction to his or her glory will always affect your intimacy. Your knowledge of that glory will be tightly woven into the conception of your relationship. However, on earth, God's glory is cloaked, and we are able to see Him as Father first. Because He chose to shield our view with flesh, we can forge an intimate relationship with Him by faith through Jesus. We get to know His love before we fully know His glory. We get to know Him as Father before we truly experience Him as King of the Universe.

I've begged God to show me His glory. I've asked Him time and again for Him to reveal His beauty to me. I knew He was shielding me, but I didn't know why. Now I do. He wants me to love Him as a Father, so He lovingly protects me from His glory. My faith is strengthened because I know one day my Father will reveal His glory to me, and I will rejoice from a daughter's heart who knows her Father intimately.

"After Jesus said this, he looked toward heaven and prayed: 'Father, the hour has come. Glorify your Son, that your Son may glorify you. For you granted him authority over all people that he might give eternal life to all those you have given him. Now this is eternal life: that they know you, the only true God, and Jesus Christ, whom you have sent. I have brought you glory on earth by finishing the work you gave me to do. And now, Father, glorify me in your presence with the glory I had with you before the world began'" (John17.1-5 NIV).

Kingdom Movement

Many Christians receive salvation through Christ, but they don't pursue a relationship with Him; therefore, their lives blend in with the cultural norm. Other Christians receive salvation and pursue good works rather than an intimate relationship with Christ. Good works become idols instead of outward displays of an inward fellowship.

As Christ's disciples, we are called to become like Him. We cannot become like Jesus by our own effort. It must be the Holy Spirit working in us (Philippians 1.6 and 2.13). When Christians passionately pursue an intimate relationship with Jesus, their lives will be sanctified (set-apart) and will produce God-centered good works (Ephesians 2.10 and John 17.19).

I believe God has an awesome and powerful Kingdom Purpose for each of us. What I would like to suggest is that God's Kingdom Purpose is what initially moves us towards intimacy with God. And as our intimacy with Him matures, we will become more like Christ.

God created this earth and gave us dominion over it (Genesis 1.26

and Psalm 115.16). Jesus uses the Parable of the Talents to illustrate that we will each be given a portion of His Kingdom (Matthew 25.21). Therefore, God obviously has given us a portion of control over this earth for a reason. He wants us to have territory and use our authority to expand it.

"Jabez cried out to the God of Israel, 'Oh, that you would bless me and enlarge my territory! Let your hand be with me, and keep me from harm so that I will be free from pain.' And God granted his request" (1 Chronicles 4.10 NIV).

What I'm realizing through researching the Scriptures is that our Kingdom Purpose is essential to our lives on this earth. It draws us closer to God and shapes us into the image of Christ. Sadly, though, many Christians are hopelessly kingdom-less. They have no idea why they are on this earth and, therefore, become easy prey for the enemy. We lose our focus if we haven't got a focal point.

I'm learning that the more God gives me a clearer vision of my own Kingdom Purpose, the more I draw closer to Him because I know that there is absolutely no way that I could achieve my Kingdom Purpose alone. I must keep in step with the Spirit. And this is why the Kingdom Purpose moves us towards Christlikeness—it prompts us to commune with God. If we are serving a purpose and it seems easy enough to do alone, I don't think we've reached the height of what God wants to do through us.

I believe that besides ignorance and apathy, the number one hindrance preventing us from achieving our Kingdom Purpose is covet-ness. The world has its own degrees of what is meaningful and what is not; however, this hierarchy does not fit in with God's vision. We get into trouble when we start idolizing a particular Kingdom Purpose instead of fulfilling our own. Whether we are front-porch disciple-makers or TV evangelist, we all have equal freedom to multiply our *Talents* and further God's Kingdom.

We each have God's glory waiting in us in the form of our Kingdom Purpose. We just have to obediently unleash it. This power is the greatest force that will shape us into Christlikeness. Our Kingdom Purpose can only be accomplished if we lean on God, obey His commands and desire Him more than anything. When we accomplish all that God has planned for us on earth, He will reward us in heaven.

"His master replied, 'Well done, good and faithful servant! You have been faithful with a few things; I will put you in charge of many things. Come and share your master's happiness!'" (Matthew 25.21 NIV).

Electric Predestination

God gave us life, and He gave us free will. With our free will we made choices of good (love, forgiveness, giving, etc.), but we also made choices of evil (hate, envy, selfishness, etc.). Our ungodly choices caused sin to enter the world, and God's perfect creation was corrupted. But along with free will, God gave us Jesus Christ, thereby redeeming the evil He knew that some of our actions would produce.

Free will is our Keys to the Kingdom; we can use these Keys to "bind" and "loose" into God's creation. "I will give you the keys of the kingdom of heaven; whatever you bind on earth will be bound in heaven, and whatever you loose on earth well be loosed in heaven" (Matthew 16.19 NIV).

The flow of the Holy Spirit in our lives is dependent on our acceptance of it. God has a purpose for our lives and He promises to be with us every inch of the way, but because of free will, we have to make the first move by receiving it. We take leaps of faith into God's divine plan, and the Holy Spirit guides our steps. The Holy Spirit cannot force God's children into submission, and that is why trust in God's Word and obedience to His promptings are vital to living out God's best.

I believe God has His best in mind for all His children. I do not believe that God "predestined" a rare, lucky few to be called to His best. That concept goes directly against free will and our ability to choose. If there wasn't free will, there wouldn't be sin in this world and the negative aspects that come along with it (pain, sorrow and death).

I do believe, though, that God is timeless and eternal (Revelation 22.13). He is past, present and future (Revelation 1.8). He is not limited to our understanding of time and space. He knows everything, but even with this knowledge, He still has given us the Keys.

"For those God foreknew he also predestined to be conformed to the image of his Son, that he might be the firstborn among many brothers and sisters. And those he predestined, he also called; those he called, he also justified; those he justified, he also glorified" (Romans 8.29-30 NIV).

I imagine that when God created life, His predestination went out like an electrical current of anointing that extended over our world, and it stopped at anyone willing to receive its charge. However, much like a lightbulb, the switch had to be flipped to the on position. God sent out a call to all His children to receive His anointing, but they needed to be willing to receive it.

Automatically, when God sent out His call, He could see the end result of those who accepted this invitation because He is not limited to space and time. In essence, we all have been predestined, but only the ones who accept the call will walk in that pre-planned destiny. These people become much like lightbulbs—individuals who allow themselves to be filled with the electricity of God's anointing.

Because God "foreknew" who would accept His call, He was able to "predestine" them, but that doesn't change the fact that everyone has been given the call. God wants all His children to be plugged into His Kingdom and His purposes on earth.

The fact that He knows the end results does not negate the free will we have to respond. In the Bible, God gave His children many chances through the prophets to repent and accept His amazing plan, even when He knew they would repeatedly reject those invitations. Even Jesus prayed for Simon (Peter) that his faith would not fail, all the while knowing it would fail and that Peter would have to repent.

"Simon, Simon, Satan has asked to sift all of you as wheat. But I have prayed for you, Simon, that your faith may not fail. And when you have turned back, strengthen your brothers" (Luke 22.31-32 NIV).

Knowing Peter would fail did not prevent Jesus from praying that he wouldn't. The chance is given even if the end result is known. God is all-knowing, but He is also all-loving, and His the current of His call goes out to be rejected or received. Yet God is the God of infinite chances. It is never too late to repent and accept His invitation.

"Yet I still dare to hope when I remember this: The faithful love of the Lord never ends! His mercies never cease" (Lamentations 3.21-22 NLT).

God's anointing is like electricity, flowing throughout this world, seeking anyone willing to receive it. He is all around us, and His call to all His children to be "predestined" for His greatness is everywhere. He wants the best for all of us, but we need to use our free will to accept and walk in it. If we do open ourselves to Him, He will fill us with the electricity of His anointing, so we can light up this dark world with the light of Jesus Christ.

"For the eyes of the LORD range throughout the earth to strengthen those whose hearts are fully committed to him…" (2 Chronicles 16.9 NIV).

A Church United

Jesus communicates with a variety of people in the New Testament; and His speech, attitude and commands appear to contradict with each interaction He makes. But instead of noticing these contradictions and analyzing their purpose, we cling to a few interactions that seem acceptable to us and fit our design. Then we expect everyone to live by it no matter who they are. We watch as Jesus commands the rich man to sell all His possessions and give the money to the poor (Luke 18.22), and our hearts begin to unknowingly or knowingly judge all those with money.

"They are not being obedient to God's command," we think. All the while we fail to recognize that Jesus encountered other individuals with money, yet He never required this act of sacrifice from them.

Jesus meets Zacchaeus in Jericho and invites Himself to Zacchaeus's house for dinner. Zacchaeus is a tax collector and has become rich from taking money from the poor. Jesus never asks Zacchaeus to sell all his processions. Zacchaeus hears people criticizing him, so he stands up and declares that he will give half his money to the poor and pay back those he has cheated. This is an amazing sacrifice, but it's definitely not what Jesus commanded from the rich man earlier in the chapter. Jesus commanded all his money be given. However, Jesus says salvation has come to the house of Zacchaeus, even though he didn't fulfill the entire command Jesus gave previously (Luke 19.1-9).

Or we become confused when Jesus interacts with the Gentile (non-Jewish) woman whose daughter is demon-possessed. She begs Jesus for a miracle, yet He tells her something that might be considered offensive, "It is not right to take the children's bread and toss it to the dogs" (Matthew 15.26 NIV). This interaction is in stark contrast to Jesus' encounter with another Gentile, the Centurion. This soldier asks Jesus to help his servant who is paralyzed, and Jesus instantly says He will go heal him (Matthew 8.5-8).

Why is Jesus treating the two Gentiles differently? One is a Canaanite, the other Roman. One is a woman, the other a man. One has no worldly significance, the other a leader in a powerful military. Is Jesus showing partiality? No, the Bible explains that Jesus would not want us to show partiality to His people (James 2.1) and God does not show favoritism (Acts 10.34-35).

What are some other seeming contradictions?

Jesus tells the man wanting to bury his father to follow Him and "let the dead bury their own dead" (Matthew 8.22 NIV). Yet during a funeral procession, Jesus' heart is moved, and He brings the widow's only son back to life (Luke 7.11-16). Moreover, Jesus weeps for Lazarus and goes to his tomb to bring him back from the dead (John 11.38-44).

Jesus tells the parable of the King who becomes a poor stranger without food, drink, shelter and clothing; and the people who do not help Him will be judged (Matthew 25.34-46). Yet when one of Jesus' disciples accuses Him of wasting one year's worth of wages on perfume that should have been given to the poor, Jesus says, "You will always have the poor among you, but you will not always have me" (John 12.8 NIV).

Jesus calls the religious leaders vipers, hypocrites and sons of the Devil (Matthew 12.34, Matthew 23.13 and John 8.44 NIV), but Jesus willingly meets with a religious leader, Nicodemus, in the cover of night to discuss faith (John 3.1-2).

Why does Jesus seem to treat every person differently?

He feeds 4,000 (Mark 8.1-10), yet He doesn't help His hungry disciples who realize that they only have one loaf of bread between them (Mark 8.14-17).

He heals a blind man with mud (John 9.6), yet He heals Bartimaeus without touching Him (Mark 10.46-52).

He speaks to the crowd in parables (Matthew 13.34), yet He explains those parables to His disciples (Matthew 13.36).

And the list goes on. Why do Jesus' actions seem to change depending on who is interacting with Him?

The answer to Jesus' movements is simple: Jesus (one of the Persons of our Triune God) knows the heart of each of us, and He knows the best way to strip us of our sins, idols and fears; so He can meet us on our level where we can receive His truth best. "He said to them, 'You are the ones who justify yourselves in the eyes of others, but God knows your hearts. What people value highly is detestable in God's sight'" (Luke 16.15 NIV). We can't fully anticipate Jesus' movements because only He can fully discern the hearts of people.

And what we value higher than God is different for each of us.

Some people value money, power, fame, security, laziness, food, appearance, bitterness, acts of service, intellect, comfort, youth, influence, affirmation, glory and other people more than they value God; and Jesus shot right to the heart of the issue. He altered His presentation of truth, so the people listening could better understand and receive it. But He never alters Truth. The Holy Spirit may move, but Truth never changes.

We learn from Jesus' interactions that we must not allow ourselves to put a blanket command on everyone. Not only does a single church have different parts, the entire Body of Christ (the Church) has different parts.

"Just as a body, though one, has many parts, but all its many parts form one body, so it is with Christ. For we were all baptized by one Spirit so as to form one body—whether Jews or Gentiles, slave or free—and we were all given the one Spirit to drink. Even so the body is not made up of one part but many" (1 Corinthians 12.12-14 NIV).

I see many Christian leaders wanting a Church unification, but too often they are seeking Church homogenization (making everyone the same). A church pastor, congregation and movement will be different in Georgia, different in California, different in Texas, different in Korea, different in the Middle East, different in South America and different in Africa because the people in those different areas are being led into God's Kingdom through Christ in unique ways that apply to them socially, demographically and personally.

We add guilt onto people when we expect them to live out our

God-ordained purposes, and we become thieves by trying to rob them of the purpose God has for them. The one injustice about mass communication is that people may be reading, hearing or seeing a movement of God not designed for them.

Christians are becoming so confused by all the finger-pointing and name-calling within the Body of Christ, and this confusion is immobilizing them in fear and preventing them from living a life of faith. But if we would all do what God has set before us while encouraging our sisters and brothers to find their center in Christ in whatever season of life, field of service or movement in which they find themselves, we would be a united force in this world.

A Kingdom divided falls (Matthew 12.25 NIV). When Christian leaders judge, bash and criticize other Christian leaders for the way God's leading them, they tear apart the Body of Christ. There is nothing wrong with promoting our God-ordained purposes; but we can do it without accusing others of indifference, fruitlessness and disobedience.

We must ignite passion without igniting shame! God wants all of His children to enter the Wedding Feast of Christ, and He will use different people and different tactics without compromising His Word to get His children to accept salvation through Jesus because He loves us that much (Matthew 22.1-14).

Glean the gold from the Christian leaders you find on TV, Online or in books; but do not allow their agenda to make you question what God is doing in your life and what He is calling you to do. The Holy Spirit in your heart takes precedence over the most skilled speaker, dynamic leader and awesome writer.

People can encourage you on your path, but they must not create your path—only the Holy Spirit can do that. And when God gives you a passion burning in your heart to fulfill a need in His Kingdom on earth, don't make it your mission to make everyone like you. We are all (ministries and individuals) different parts in the United Church, and only by working together, can we fulfill God's awesome Kingdom Plan on earth as it is in heaven.

"I appeal to you, dear brothers and sisters, by the authority of our Lord Jesus Christ, to live in harmony with each other. Let there be no divisions in the church. Rather, be of one mind, united in thought and purpose" (1 Corinthians 1.10 NLT).

The Harvest

I struggle with judging people and ministries trying to reach the world for Christ. I remember hearing a Christian techno song once. I liked the song, but I imagined it being played at some rave party, while the underaged kids danced with ecstasy streaming through their veins. I thought to myself, "How could this song possibly lead someone to Christ?"

I envisioned the seeds of the Gospel being scattered all over the party, sowing God's truth in fruitless efforts. "All those seeds go to waste," I told God.

"Not all of them," He replied.

Then I saw a girl in my mind's eye. She woke up depressed and hung over. She remembered dancing to a song about Jesus the night before. She thought it was weird at the time, but now she wanted to know more. She searched her mother's room for a Bible and while reading it, the Holy Spirit brought her to the cross. Saved by a techno Christian song!

Another time I judged was when I saw a man drag a cross up and down the beach. "There are so many more productive ways to reach people for Christ," I thought. "At most, he might reach a few in one day." Then I heard an amazing pastor talk at a conference. He was saved by a man who dragged a cross up and down the local street where his parents owned a beach rental store. The pastor now reaches thousands for Christ. Saved by a man dragging a cross!

I'm realizing that God reaches into the deserts of people's hearts with His grace to touch the lives of His lost children. If every person has his or her own desert, then there are billions of deserts in this world that God wants to bring His mercy to. Each of us has deserts within walking distance of our individual lives. We can't focus with jealousy or judgment on what other people and ministries are doing. We need to look around and enter those desert places closest to us with God's love and truth. The harvest is plentiful, but the workers are few because people are all distracted focusing on what everyone else is doing.

So whether a ministry is small or large, cutting edge or traditional, local or overseas, individual or cooperate, we should pray for them but keep our eyes focused on the fields that God has placed before us to cultivate. We will do no good trying to analyze the steps of others and their ministries. And quite frankly, it's exhausting and time-consuming worrying about what everyone else is doing. We need to thoughtfully ask God what desert He wants us to reach, and then plow that desert like we only have a vapor of time left to finish it.

"Then he [Jesus] said to his disciples, 'The harvest is plentiful but the workers are few. Ask the Lord of the harvest, therefore, to send out workers into his harvest field'" (Matthew 9.37-38 NIV).

Bartimaeus's Gumption

Bartimaeus, a blind beggar, heard that Jesus was arriving. A crowd surrounded Jesus, so Bartimaeus yelled, "Jesus, Son of David, have mercy on me!" (Luke 18.38 NIV). Many of the people Jesus healed were brought to Him by friends, but not Bartimaeus. Instead of helping him, the crowd told him to be quiet.

But Bartimaeus did not let his blindness and the lack of help stop him from calling out to Jesus. He couldn't see, but he could yell. So he yelled even louder, "Son of David, have mercy on me!" The title "Son of David" alludes to the Messiah: "Out of the stump of David's family will grow a shoot— yes, a new Branch bearing fruit from the old root" (Isaiah 11.1 NLT). Bartimaeus knew that the Messiah was in his presence, and he was determined to reach Him.

Jesus picked Bartimaeus's voice out from the crowd and called him over. Bartimaeus threw aside his coat (probably the most expensive thing he owned), jumped up and ran to Jesus. Jesus asked him what he wanted, and Bartimaeus said, "My rabbi, I want to see!" Instantly, Bartimaeus was healed, and he followed

Jesus (Mark 10.46-52).

My husband read me this story a few nights ago, and I couldn't help but feel encouraged. Bartimaeus didn't have sight, but he had a voice and he used it. When no one would see for him and lead him to Christ, he used the resources at his disposal. Bartimaeus's voice might not have sounded the best, but he used it with power and determination. He focused all his energy on Jesus and found himself at the foot of love, mercy and grace.

My weakness is my voice. I have nodules on my vocals cords, so I'm not supposed to yell, sing or talk too much. However, I have three young kids, and I find myself losing my voice a lot. I have to tell my oldest son—who happens to ask a lot of questions—that I have to take a break from talking because my throat hurts. I can't sing at church. I can't holler when I'm excited. I can't read out loud to my kids or talk on the phone very long. I have to be careful to conserve my voice because I don't have much of it to spare.

Since I can't use my physical voice to call out to Jesus, I write. My writing may not be the best, but I will use it to reach Jesus. I will not let the negative jeers of the crowd cause me to give up. Jesus tells me to come to Him, and I let go of all my desires so that I can run to the foot of His love, mercy and grace. I know He'll give me a voice to call attention to Him, and I will use it to praise God and give Him glory!

"They were just trying to intimidate us, imagining that they could discourage us and stop the work. I continued the work with even greater determination" (Nehemiah 6.9 NLT).

Pruning Shears

Allowing God to expose and extract sin is one of the most difficult yet rewarding procedures of the Christian life. I have found that this process is especially painful when the sin is deeply rooted in selfishness, pride and entitlement. The hardest sin for God to pull from me is the sin that I wasn't even aware I had. God would take hold of the ugly weed, and I'd wallow in a mire of denial, pity and shock. A spiritual tug-of-war would commence, and I'd struggle with allowing the sharp (but quick) pruning of God's hand.

The most recent weed uprooting took place just a few weeks ago. A situation compressed with just the right elements brought to the forefront an incognito, tightly fastened and fully entitled sin of mine. This particular sin only shows up when the atmosphere is drenched with my supposed suffering and misfortune, and I find myself working in defense mode. Instead of claiming my rights and holding onto my justifications this time, God brought me to my knees with reality. No matter where the division of blame lies, I had to claim the sin that sat in my corner.

I wanted to focus on all the other ingredients of the mess, but God sifted through the bowl and handed me my portion of blame. BLAH! I yelled to God, "Why must I be the only one to claim responsibility? Why must I be the only one to humble myself? Why must I be the only one committed to Your correction?" (None of those statements were true, but that is exactly how I felt at the time.)

Finally, I prayed for God to help me, and I took that weed out and laid it at the cross. Instantly, I was filled with the most amazing peace and satisfaction, and I felt righteous before the eyes of my Creator. God's healing and love covered me, and the presence of the Holy Spirit filled me even more. The entire process from the time I started feeling the pressure of God's hand to the actual removal of my entrenched sin only took a single evening, but it was a miserable journey that, thankfully, ended in a pool of grace.

I used to wonder what it meant to be filled and led by the Holy Spirit, but now I know. The Spirit of God dwells only in the parts of our hearts that have been surrendered to Him. The more sin that God is able to extract, the more places the Holy Spirit can fill. A person who is filled to the brim with the Holy Spirit is a person who has had a lot of sin exposed and pulled.

When God reveals the dark parts of our hearts, He's trying to secure more living space for His Spirit. So now when I feel God's pruning shears coming, I can be ready with the knowledge that the painful procedure will be over soon, and the tender area will be generously soaked in God's healing peace and presence.

"Whoever heeds life-giving correction will be at home among the wise" (Proverbs 15.31 NIV).

Water Sting

I've been learning jiu-jitsu—a type of grappling that teaches you how to put your opponent into submission. I enjoy my training because it gives me a great work out and empowers me with simple self-defense techniques. The main problem I've encountered (aside from sore muscles) is that you can get mat burn. I've discovered these abrasions on my back, feet, elbows and knees. You don't notice them right away because you are so focused on your training. However, you definitely feel them once you get into the shower.

When the water rolls over the parts of your body that are missing their top layer of skin, you experience sharp stinging sensations. The first time I suffered through this painful shower drama, I thought scorpions were stinging me. Now, every time I get in the shower after some groundwork, I prepare myself for the burning stings. But I know that if I don't wash off my abrasions, they will get infected and cause major problems to my body. The pain is a necessary part of my cleansing.

Throughout the Bible, Jesus is compared to Living Water. Water has many amazing qualities, which include cleansing. Jesus desires to purify us and wash us clean; however, it is not always a pleasant process. In fact, when we let Jesus wash over our wounds, it can cause us serious and intense pain. But if we don't let His presence pour into every part of who we are, our past and current hurts will begin to harm us, stealing all the good God wants to bless us with.

The first time we let Jesus expose our wounds, we might be shocked by how much it hurts. However, when we allow the healing process to come to completion, we understand that the pain was necessary to our recovery. Now every time we get hurt, we know that the sting only lasts for a moment; but the joy, peace and healing we gain last a lifetime. The faster we reveal our wounds, the faster Jesus is able to heal us, giving us new hearts that please Him.

"Then I will sprinkle clean water on you, and you will be clean. Your filth will be washed away, and you will no longer worship idols. And I will give you a new heart, and I will put a new spirit in you. I will take out your stony, stubborn heart and give you a tender, responsive heart" (Ezekiel 63.25-26 NLT).

God has a great purpose for each of us, and He wants to shine His glory through our lives. By accepting Jesus' payment for our sins and taking on His righteousness, we have become new creations by faith. And God will continue to perfect us until we transform into the beautiful people He created us to be from the inside out. But we must stay submitted to the healing process that scrubs away the tarnishes of sin. Because of grace, we have become members of a Divine Family, and God desires to make His children into the glorious image of His Son.

"It makes good sense that the God who got everything started and keeps everything going now completes the work by making the Salvation Pioneer perfect through suffering as he leads all these people to glory. Since the One who saves and those who are saved have a common origin, Jesus doesn't hesitate to treat them as family, saying, I'll tell my good friends, my brothers and sisters, all I know about you; I'll join them in worship and praise to you. Again, he puts himself in the same family circle when he says, Even I live by placing my trust in God. And yet again, I'm here with the children God gave me" (Hebrews 2.10-13 MSG).

Buying Land

I love reading the parables about the Kingdom of Heaven. The Bible says that as Believers in Christ, the Kingdom of Heaven is in us (Luke 17.21). We receive righteousness when we accept Jesus' sacrifice for our sins, and we become blameless so that a perfect God can dwell inside of us by means of the Holy Spirit.

Once we have the Holy Spirit, the entire Kingdom of Heaven is at our disposal. We don't have to wait until our mortal bodies die! It is a wonderful truth that is contrary to our culture's worldview of "you must earn everything," "you must see it to believe it," and "God is beyond your reach."

I love the parable that compares the Kingdom of Heaven to a treasure found it a field; however, I finally asked a question that the Holy Spirit used to give me new insight. I asked, "Why did the man have to buy the field? Why couldn't he just take the treasure?" The Holy Spirit said, "Sometimes the Kingdom of Heaven can only be found in the land."

What I realized is that we all have different "fields" in our lives: our marriages, children, work, church, time, money, talents, relationships, habits, etc. And God has treasures for us that can only be found in those particular landscapes. So many people want God, but what they don't realize is that God is found in everything, and it is only when we sacrifice all that we have to buy those "fields" that we are able to dig up the treasures God has for us.

When we sacrifice our time to read the Bible, we will find treasure.

When we sacrifice our self-centered control for the sake of marital harmony, we will find treasure.

When we sacrifice our energy to pour into our children, we will find treasure.

When we sacrifice our material wants to give to our church and others, we will find treasure.

When we sacrifice our clean homes to cultivate our relationships, we will find treasure.

I believe some aspects of the Kingdom of God are like pearls, given to us freely by our Creator (Matthew 13.45-46). However, much of the treasure can only be found in the fields where God has planted them. And they almost always take a lot of digging, sweat and work to discover.

So if God is calling you to cultivate a field and you wonder how it will bring you closer to Him, don't worry. I'm sure there is a treasure just waiting to be found. And once you find it, you will joyfully continue to dig more because the treasure was well worth the sacrifice. The amazing thing is that the treasure always brings you into a deeper relationship with Christ because He is the Treasure!

"The kingdom of heaven is like treasure hidden in a field. When a man found it, he hid it again, and then in his joy went and sold all he had and bought that field" (Matthew 13.44 NIV).

Riding Out the Storm

Hikers know that when a storm hits, it is time to find a secure place to wait it out: "If the storm is truly awful and you can't count on getting anymore hiking done, resign yourself to the fact and set your camp up for the evening" (*The Complete Idiot's Guide to Camping and Hiking* by Michael Mouland). Bad weather comes with high winds, rain, hail and lightning—all which can make you wish you never went camping in the first place.

The worst thing you can do is desperately run into the powerful clutches of nature, hoping to find a ray of sunshine in the chaos. Storms are intense, but they usually don't last long. Instead of questioning the storm or grieving its presence, make yourself cozy and ride it out with the understanding that storms are a part of life.

The expression "riding out the storm" gives me a better perspective for spiritual storms. Just like physical weather systems, there are also spiritual weather systems (Ephesians 6.12). And I've noticed that when my eyes are intently on God, He will let me know when the climate is primed for a spiritual storm.

In the past when I was under spiritual attack, I would fight it. I'd run wildly around looking for answers. I'd questioned the angry clouds. I'd challenge the pounding hail. I'd shake my fist at lightening. I'd confront the storm, and then drag my weary, battered and confused self back home. If God has given me authority to withstand such attacks, why was I getting pulverized (Luke 10.19)?

Finally, I felt the Holy Spirit tell me to stop fighting the storm and just make camp and wait it out. What a revolutionary thought! God provides us times to learn and grow, but a spiritual storm is not one of those times. During a spiritual storm, we need to dig in our heels, secure our roots in Christ and strengthen our spiritual core.

When Jesus was under spiritual attack in the wilderness, He stayed still and brought forth the Word that was stored up in His heart. Instead of seeking understanding, I should have stayed still and remembered all that God has already taught me.

I realized that all the enemy was trying to do during a spiritual attack was to make me react impulsively in fear. When the devil attacked Jesus in the wilderness, he tried to make Jesus react:

1) Turn the stones into bread (Matthew 4.3).
2) Throw Himself off the temple (Matthew 4.6).
3) Worship the devil (Matthew 4.9).

Sometimes the best thing you can do when under spiritual attack is to BE STILL (Psalm 46.10). Many times, I'd randomly opened my Bible, sought advice from others or even Googled my question into the Internet abyss only to become more confused. I know that these methods have helped me in the past during a season of growth, but they were no help in the face of a storm. Continue faithfully praying and reading your Bible, but stay low and make no move until the wind eases up and the rain stops pouring. You'll find clarity once the sun comes out again.

The storm is designed to move us into confusion and make us do things we will regret. Our movements will be spurred by fear, doubt, hurt, fatigue, anxiety, confusion and other negative emotions; and the damage caused by our foolish, impulsive actions will be seen everywhere once the storm breaks. Rather than running wildly about like panicky lunatics, we need to stay still and recall all of God's promises stored up in our hearts.

So if all you know is that God sent His Only Son so we can have everlasting life (John 3.16) or that we can do all things through Christ who gives us strength (Philippians 4.13), repeat those promises over and over again until the weather clears. And after the storm ends, devour God's Word for more promises so that when the next storm hits, you'll be better prepared to take refuge in Him.

"If you say, 'The LORD is my refuge,' and you make the Most High your dwelling, no harm will overtake you, no disaster will come near your tent" (Psalm 91.9-10 NIV).

Beautiful, Dirty Feet

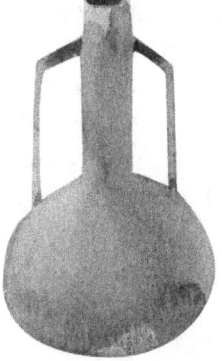

"How beautiful on the mountains are the feet of the messenger who brings good news, the good news of peace and salvation, the news that the God of Israel reigns!" (Isaiah 52.7 NLT).

I'm in the kitchen a lot. It seems that I'm always cooking or cleaning something in that space. I think when my kids have grown, they will have an image of Mom standing in front of the sink or the stove. The kitchen has become one of my main sources of service to my family.

My kitchen floor is made up of rugged blue stones that hide any evidence of dirt or stains. I love to kick off my shoes and stand on the cool floor with my bare feet. I've probably worn a path from the fridge to the trashcan to the sink to the stove, since I walk that circuit often.

I've noticed, however, that my feet collect dirt during my hours of pacing the short length of my kitchen. My entire body is clean and fresh, but my feet look like they haven't been washed in days. I don't mind, though, because that is the price I pay to care for my family. Before I leave my kitchen duties, I stick my feet in the sink to clean them. Otherwise, I'd track dirty footprints throughout the rest of my house.

I pondered this as I read about Jesus washing His disciples' feet. I was struck when He told them that they (except for Judas who betrayed Jesus) were all clean besides their feet: "Jesus replied, 'A person who has bathed all over does not need to wash, except for the feet, to be entirely clean. And you disciples are clean, but not all of you'" (John 13.10 NLT). I'm sure the disciples did a lot of walking while spreading the Gospel, and their feet were probably filthy from their journeys with Jesus.

I then thought about my journey. God has chosen to expose me to situations, actions and words that were disturbing to my spirit. I had trouble at first trying to digest the ugliness of what I saw and heard. I wanted to point my finger at all the ungodliness around me; but if I did, I would never be able to reach others with the Good News of Jesus Christ—it is hard to be open to someone who is attacking you.

Instead of attacking, I had to put on the Shoes of Peace (Ephesians 6.15). I looked past the sin into the hearts of people who needed a Savior. We all have sin, but it is difficult to trek through the muddy waters of another person's mistakes, ignorance and deception. I spoke of God's grace and love, but I began to feel dirty and tainted. I desperately needed Jesus to wash my feet before they started making tracks throughout the rest of my life.

Jesus and His disciples hung around "disreputable sinners" (Mark 2.15 NLT). I believe that Jesus—being the Son of God and a sinless man—saw the ugliness of sin all around Him. But instead of calling it out, He chose to show grace. When the Pharisees saw Jesus eating with His followers, they asked, "Why does he eat with such scum?" (Mark 2.16 NLT).

Jesus answered, "Healthy people don't need a doctor—sick people do. I have come to call not those who think they are righteous, but those who know they are sinners" (Mark 2.17 NLT).

I'm reminded that Jesus left His flawless glory to come to earth and get His feet dirty, so He could offer us the hope of salvation. He exposed Himself to "sick people"—even taking our sins on Himself—and sacrificed His life so we could be blameless in God's sight: "He made Him who knew no sin to be sin on our behalf, so that we might become the righteousness of God in Him" (2 Corinthians 5.21 NASB).

I've noticed that as a disciple of Jesus Christ, my feet will get dirty. God will send me into the trenches; and although my heart stays pure and right, my feet will become filthy and worn. But I can't let a little dirt stop me from spreading the Gospel. If I fear getting my feet dirty, I will never be God's productive co-worker with Christ. I want to follow Jesus' example—He didn't judge others: "For God did not send the Son into the world to judge the world, but that the world might be saved through Him" (John 3.17 NASB).

I must prepare my feet for the dirt with the understanding that I can keep my heart and mind clean. I can't worry about the opinions of those who care more about staying sanitized than about reaching the lost. I know that Jesus will always wash my feet when they get dirty, and I trust that He will use my feet to share the Good News!

"So also Jesus suffered and died outside the city gates to make his people holy by means of his own blood. So let us go out to him, outside the camp, and bear the disgrace he bore. For this world is not our permanent home; we are looking forward to a home yet to come" (Hebrews 13.12-14 NLT).

Crushed

"Jesus replied, 'Now the time has come for the Son of Man to enter into his glory. I tell you the truth, unless a kernel of wheat is planted in the soil and dies, it remains alone. But its death will produce many new kernels—a plentiful harvest of new lives'" (John 12.23-24 NLT).

As I headed to the department store, I saw a seagull sitting in the middle of the parking lot. I walked by him, and he barely moved. He rested in the center of traffic. "He's going to get hurt," I thought. But the Holy Spirit reminded me of Jesus' words that God protects the little birds (Matthew 6.26), so I quickly bought what I needed from the store and went back to my car. I scanned for the seagull, and my eyes widen when I saw him. He was crushed. A car ran over the lower half of his body, and pieces of his yellow legs and wings were scattered around him. I didn't understand what God was trying to teach me, but I kept my heart open even though the sight was extremely upsetting.

Later, I was driving to my sister's house, and I saw several black birds huddled together on the street. They surrounded a comrade that had just gotten run over. Again, I thought about the Scripture of God's protection, and I told myself that if I saw one more bird, I would know that the Holy Spirit was definitely showing me something. That evening as I was leaving the gym, I saw a beautiful cormorant duck sitting by the curb of the parking lot. He looked confused and lost. I drove by him hoping he would take flight, but he slowly waddled closer to the edge. He was dying and could no longer fly away.

If God loved these beautiful creatures, how could they die so miserably? I found my answer in the Gospels. During this time my mood was especially somber. I was coming up to Jesus' death on the cross in my yearly Bible reading, and I wasn't looking forward to it. I knew what was about to happen. Jesus would be crushed for the freedom of God's children designed in His image. My mood worsened with the Christmas holiday because we celebrate the birth of Jesus: the perfect Baby born to save us. But the flip side to His divine birth is the inevitability of His horrific death.

I started to notice a theme, however, as Jesus' time to die came closer. When Jesus prophesied about His death, He would simultaneously prophesy about His glory. It seemed that the ugliness of death was a precursor for supernatural glory. And a thought struck me: When that seagull lay dismembered on the ground, did God's unseen glory shine through? Was the bird's essence tucked away as a seed for the New Earth (Isaiah 65.17 and Revelation 21.1)? Is there a beautiful aspect to death that can only be realized by faith?

Then I thought about all life. Parents across the globe welcome their beautiful babies into this world with the knowledge that their bundles of joy will be crushed one day. A car, an illness, an accident or old age will eventually destroy their lives. No one is exempt from the gruesome hand of death. We all will be crushed; and if our hearts are not set on God and eternity, this existence can seem like a cruel joke instead of the gateway to our real lives.

Even Mary's excitement over Jesus' birth must have been dampened by the prophet's words of the sorrow she'd feel when He would be crucified: "Then Simeon blessed them and said to Mary, his mother: 'This child is destined to cause the falling and rising of many in Israel, and to be a sign that will be spoken against, so that the thoughts of many hearts will be revealed. And a sword will pierce your own soul too' (Luke 2.34-35 NIV).

All life ends in death, but Jesus' life gives us so much hope because He chose to die alongside us. And His death is a seed that births our future glory—a glory that begins once our physical bodies are crushed. However, we must have faith to believe it and trust to claim it.

Jesus gave a simple promise to the man hanging on his own cross of death next to Him: "Jesus answered him, 'Truly I tell you, today you will be with me in paradise'" (Luke 23.43 NIV). Life ends bleakly on this earth. We will all be like those birds—we will disappear from existence and people years from now will walk over our graves. We will die in pain, crushed and forgotten.

And although there is no proof or evidence to the glory Jesus claimed and the paradise He professed, I choose to whole heartily believe. I base my life on Jesus' promises, and I trust there is more to this existence than birth, death and a little in between. My spirit longs to live forever, and I know God has planted eternity in my heart (Ecclesiastes 3.11).

Now when I see the Baby Jesus in the manger, I'm reminded that my Creator chose to experience the excruciating sting of death with me. I'm not alone, and I don't have to be scared. As I draw closer to Jesus and stay my gaze on Him, I begin to see that this earth is not my true home. This life is only a shadow of the beautiful New Earth that God is preparing for us—an earth where sin can no longer cause us pain, sorrow and fear (Hebrews 11.14-16). We will never be separated from the presence of God and the awesome attributes of His glory, and He will gather His blood-soaked creation in His arms and see only the righteousness of His Son.

I desire to confidently reiterate the Apostle Paul's words: "For to me, to live is Christ and to die is gain" (Philippians 1.21 NIV). To die IS GAIN! I will remind myself that only when a seed dies, will the full harvest of life be realized. As I mourn seeds of death around me, I will profess the crop of unseen Glory that's produced in the paradise of our eternal lives.

Eternal Echoes

"Truly I say to you, whatever you bind on earth shall have been bound in heaven; and whatever you loose on earth shall have been loosed in heaven" (Matthew 18.18 NASB).

One afternoon, I found myself driving solo in my car, which is rare for a mommy of three young kids. When I'm alone, my thoughts tend to consume me and I'll begin to talk to myself. I started thinking about God and how much He loves me. He gave me free will, which corrupted His beautiful design, so He poured His Perfect Spirit into flesh and died for me on a cross.

Jesus redeemed my imperfections, and the Holy Spirit encourages me to continue using my God-breathed imagination within the limitless possibilities of my free will to give glory to God. My sins are covered by the blood of Jesus, and all God sees is the beautiful fulfillment of my purpose. I know I will make mistakes, but I claim grace and walk boldly to His Throne of Mercy (Hebrews 4.16). My confidence and security rest in God's faithfulness alone, and I eagerly hunger for all of His promises found in His Word, the Bible.

As I contemplated how blessed I truly am to be an adored daughter of the King of the Universe, I couldn't help but cry out my praise and honor to Him. I shouted my adorations so loudly that I was glad that all the windows were tightly rolled up because my boisterous proclamations gushed into the air. Peace, joy and love overwhelmed me. My faith no longer felt uncomfortable or weird because I firmly believe I have found the Truth to all life—we are all beautiful creations beloved by our Creator!

As I yelled out my praise, an image of heaven flashed in my mind. I could see myself kneeling at the Throne of Glory. I was surrounded by others also shouting and worshipping God. The glory of God surrounded us, and the desire to give Him honor and praise became automatic. But there was something special about my praise—all the times I shouted glory to God by faith on earth echoed in my voice in heaven.

Every verbal belief I let loose on earth was also let loose in eternity. In heaven, I no longer needed faith to see God's glory, but all the proclamations of faith I shouted because of my choice to believe gave emphasis, weight and power to my eternal expression.

We all have free will. Jesus died to give it to us. Though there is much good we can do with it, we must never forget to praise our God by faith. We were created to worship. We can choose to worship many things; but only when we worship our Creator, will we find our true joy (Psalm 43.4). So let us let loose our worship by faith on earth, so that eternity will echo with our praises of glorious belief!

"You love him even though you have never seen him. Though you do not see him now, you trust him; and you rejoice with a glorious, inexpressible joy. The reward for trusting him will be the salvation of your souls" (1 Peter 1.8-9 NLT).

Crazy Elevators

When God is stretching my faith, and He is asking me to take steps outside of my comfort zone, I have the same reoccurring dream—elevators. When I dream about elevators, I'm always apprehensive to walk in them. They look unstable and ready to plummet to the earth. Though my mind is screaming for me to stay away, I realize that there is no other way for me to get to my destination (regretfully, there are never any stairs in my dream). I take a deep breath and step into the elevator, relinquishing control of my life.

In my dreams, the elevators have been wobbly, forcing me to balance in the middle. The elevators have taken me up when I wanted to go down. The elevators have even left the building, soaring across the city horizon like a gondola. I slide back and forth in my floating elevator, praying that I make it to wherever I'm supposed to go. In all of my dreams, I never reach my destination. I wake up relieved that the dream is over but upset that there is never any resolution.

I wonder if Noah felt like this when He was tossed about in the Ark during a storm that seemed to never end. Or if Abraham felt like this when He walked through a Promised Land where he was the stranger. Or if David felt like this when he hid in caves from a bloodthirsty king who claimed his throne. Or if Jesus felt like this when He willingly endured the shame of our sins on the cross.

How can we have peace when we obediently walk into circumstances that test our resolve and stretch our faith? Romans 15.13 promises that there is peace in believing. If we can just hold onto our belief in God's faithfulness, in His promises and in His Word, we can claim peace that everything will turn out good for those who love Him and are committed to His purpose (Romans 8.28). Though all the circumstances around us may try to make us fear, we can stand firm in the knowledge that God's ways are beyond our imaginings (Isaiah 55.8).

I have to trust that God's plan is not limited to a man-made elevator. Though I have no idea what God may be doing, I have faith that He will show His glory in the middle of my trust. When my elevator finally makes it to its destination, my faith will be confirmed and strengthened. I will be filled with a fresh power to face my next trip of faith on another crazy elevator ride; and, hopefully, this time I will sit in complete peace instead of hanging on for dear life.

"May the God of hope fill you with all joy and peace as you trust in him, so that you may overflow with hope by the power of the Holy Spirit" (Romans 15.13 NIV).

My Trinne

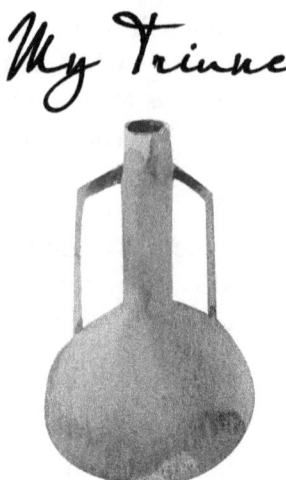

"Therefore go and make disciples of all nations, baptizing them in the name of the Father and of the Son and of the Holy Spirit, and teaching them to obey everything I have commanded you. And surely I am with you always, to the very end of the age" (Matthew 28.19-20 NIV).

When my twin sister and I were five years old and finishing our last year of pre-school, our mom signed us up for an overnight campout. Tents, food and fun were provided; and all we needed to bring was a sleeping bag and an overnight bag. I was so excited! When we arrived, my mom walked us to one of the camping attendants to check us in. After a few moments, my mom knelt and gave me the most alarming news of my young life: My twin would not be staying with me.

For the duration of my camping trip, I did not say a single word. I observed the movement around me like I was having an out of body experience. I remember watching three girls in my tent talking and laughing, and I just stared at them like a deer in headlights. One girl kept shining her flashlight at my face, and the girls would whisper and giggle. The girl finally tried to ask me a question, but I gaped and said nothing. It was as if I had been given a new set of eyes, and everything I saw was strange and dreamlike.

The next morning, I got out of my tent and stood outside until an adult asked me if I was hungry. I nodded my head, and he led me to the breakfast station. I sat alone eating pancakes, while my brain worked overtime trying to figure out if I was supposed to engage in life without my twin. Luckily, my mom came to retrieve me a few hours later. On the way home, my twin talked excitedly about all that she had done with Mom, and I sat quietly unable to understand or communicate my altered reality encounter.

As my intimacy with God grows, I've noticed that my dependency on Him has become my new reality. I can't function without relying on the Three Persons of my Creator. God is my Father. Jesus is my Savior. The Holy Spirit is my Counselor. God has beautifully chosen to interact with me in three distinct and wonderful ways; and I'm learning to know and relate with each Person of the Godhead.

God created me and knows me. He has given me a preordained purpose for my life. He loves me like a perfect parent and expects great things for me. He is Controller of the Universe, yet He cares about the small moments of my day. He wants me to give Him my worries and bring Him my prayer requests.

"Do not be anxious about anything, but in every situation, by prayer and petition, with thanksgiving, present your requests to God" (Philippians 4.6 NIV).

Jesus has been tempted with sin and carried its weight on the cross. He has walked in flesh and knows what I'm going through. He prays for me and gives me strength to live in a world and body corrupted by sin. His righteousness covers me, so I can commune with a Holy God.

"For in Christ all the fullness of the Deity lives in bodily form, and in Christ you have been brought to fullness. He is the head over every power and authority" (Colossians 2.9-10 NIV).

And because of Jesus' Finished Work on the Cross, I receive the Holy Spirit Who guides and teaches me. He unlocks the promises of the Bible and applies them to my life. He dwells within me and whispers correction and praise into my heart. He uses the stories of my life to grow me into the image of Christ.

"And I will ask the Father, and he will give you another advocate to help you and be with you forever—the Spirit of truth. The world cannot accept him, because it neither sees him nor knows him. But you know him, for he lives with you and will be in you" (John 14.16-17 NIV).

God loves me so much that He offers Himself to me in three unique ways, so that I may better know the richness of His nature. I desire my life to be so engulfed in His fullness that I'm unable to engage in living without His presence. I pray that my days are so completely wrapped up in God that every interaction, thought and word I speak has the sweet aroma of His glory and His Spirit. I want my reality to be solidly fixed on Him, so I fear His absence in my choices more than I fear the opinions of others, the impossibility of circumstance or the enormity of my faith-steps.

Firm Faith

"For we live by believing and not by seeing" (2 Corinthians 5.7 NLT).

Elihu is the younger man who proclaimed God's faithfulness to Job (Job 32.1-3) just before God revealed Himself in a whirlwind (Job 38.1). He spoke with boldness and faith about an all-powerful and mighty God, and he confronted Job's older friends with their inability to illuminate the majesty of our Creator. Elihu's daring proclamation of faith is much like the young King David when he declared victory over a giant because he believed in the faithfulness of His God (1 Samuel 17.45).

What if Elihu is the younger manifestation of Job? What if Elihu lost all he had and changed his name to Job, meaning "persecuted, hated," much like Naomi did when she told her friends to call her Mara— "bitterness" (Ruth 1.20). Scholars have suggested that Elihu is actually related to Abraham*; however, the Bible offers no lineage of Job, save his three daughters conceived in the second half of his life (Job 42.14). Wouldn't it be interesting if Elihu handed off his story of persecution and restoration to his relative, Abraham, so he could add the story of Job into the records of God's faithfulness in the Bible?

I only say this because I had my own Elihu moment. God was doing a work in me—deepening my faith. He brought me full circle to the moment many years ago when He gave me my Kingdom Promise. I had so much faith in Him then. I believed God could do anything. Of course, much of my belief was due to my ignorance. His promise for my life was planted in a world foreign to me, and I had no idea of the scope of its difficulty.

Over the course of several years, God stripped me of all my ignorance, and I become fully aware of how unfeasible it was for me to accomplish what He promised. And I struggled with clinging onto the faith I once had. I struggled with claiming God's faithfulness even in the face of impossibility. I struggled with holding onto hope even though I felt ridiculous. I struggled with believing the Word of my Father even though everything in this world said that I must have made a mistake.

I opened up my Bible and read the fresh words of Elihu, spoken in confidence to the ears of a broken man who had lost everything and questioned the faithfulness of His God. As I read Elihu's powerful declaration of faith, I saw my younger self materialize in my mind. She spoke of God's faithfulness and her belief in His promises. She walked with confidence into the purpose God established for her before time began. She demanded that I carry the weight of her faith with joy and trust even though my own experiences had shown me the impossibility of God's promise.

And God asked me, "Do you still believe as you once did?"

Will I still believe as I did so many years ago even though everything in my life says God's promise is a lie? Is my faith dependent on God's Word or the evidence surrounding me? Will

I choose to grab hold of hope or drown in disillusionment? Will I still boldly claim that God has given me a promise and He is faithful to fulfill it: "Let us hold tightly without wavering to the hope we affirm, for God can be trusted to keep his promise" (Hebrews 10.23 NLT).

God revealed Job's innermost source of his faith. He stripped Job of everything and then asked him, "Do you still believe like you once did?" Job wrestled with God for many chapters, and his friends could offer no help because they had not been exposed to the core as he was. However, Job remembered his early years when his faith was vibrant and new, and he allowed Elihu to remind him of the faith he once had.

Finally, Job could reach out to Elihu and grab hold of his faith—the purest form of it—based on nothing more than God's faithfulness alone. And in Job's brokenness He believed, and God revealed Himself to Job in a raw and untamed way. At last, Elihu could live up to his name, "My God is YAHWEH," because in the pit of his suffering, He claimed his true faith. And God fulfilled all of His promises to Job, even when circumstances left him for dead.

Before God fulfills His promises, He will test you. He will make sure that you believe in His faithfulness alone. But you have to walk down that path with Him. You must allow Him to make you uncomfortable and to strip you of any proof that your promise will come true. He will bring you to your knees and give you a choice to reject or believe Him. You must be like King David and look the Giant of Evidence in the eye and yell, "This is the LORD's battle, and he will give you to us!" (1 Samuel 17.47 NLT).

"The life of faith can take comfort from a word, and rest a world upon a promise." - Cecil

* "Then Elihu son of Barakel the Buzite, of the clan of Ram, became angry. He was angry because Job refused to admit that he had sinned and that God was right in punishing him" (Job 32.2 NLT).

"[Elihu's] His Country. 'The Buzite.' Buz the second son of Nahor, Abraham's brother (Gen. xxii. 21)" (The Preacher's Homiletic Commentary. 1996 Baker Books. Volume 10. Page 202).

Mirages in the Wilderness

Inferior mirage: "A spurious image of an object formed below the true position of that object by abnormal refraction conditions along the line of sight; one of the most common types of mirage, and the opposite of a superior mirage."

In my path to God's purpose for my life, I've chased many mirages. Glimmers of what I thought were His best appeared before me, giving me refreshed hope and inner diligence to keep on going. I'd chase down the optical allusion—my view distorted by the crippled eyes of human nature—only to find that my desired oasis evaporated in the desert sun.

I'd cry in despair and question a God who would allow such disappointment, not realizing I moved closer to His eternal throne. I'd fall flat in the desert sand, finally allowing my broken heart to be soothed by a Father rich in mercy and love.

These were my "inferior mirages" of faith, permitted by my Father to shape me into the image of Christ and bring me into intimacy with Him. These images were my attempts to refract the light of God's purpose, eager to circumvent His timeline and the invaluable process of Walking the Wilderness.

I realize now that God's arms hovered beautifully over my mirages, and He used my own selfish desires to prompt me closer to my Promised Land. By God's grace my eyes slowly lifted from the empty mirage to the sky of His majesty and love, and my footing found strength in the worship and glory of God alone.

"God has condescended by this religious commerce, to bind us to Himself more firmly by means of our wants and our desires. He desires to impress upon our minds the truth that He rules in the least events of our lives, and, by this kind of contract that He makes with us in vows, He would awaken our faith by accepting the conditions that we offer, and in accomplishing that which we expect of Him." – Le Maistre de Sacy

Superior mirage: "A spurious image of an object formed above the object's position by abnormal refraction conditions; opposite to an inferior mirage."

We must be careful not to allow our mirages to be our focus above our relationship with God. When we chase our own selfish desires with no concern at all with the will of God, we will Wander the Wilderness—never deepening our relationship with God and never getting closer to our Promised Land.

We will jump from one unsanctioned "superior mirage" to the next without growing in wisdom and understanding, and we may give up and head back home to the security of slavery.

Fata Morgana: "an unusual and complex form of mirage, a form of superior mirage, which is seen in a narrow band right above the horizon. It is an Italian phrase derived from the vulgar Latin for 'fairy' and the Arthurian sorceress Morgan le Fay, from a belief that the mirage, often seen in the Strait of Messina, were fairy castles in the air or false land designed to lure sailors to their death created by her witchcraft."

We waste the Wilderness when we begin to chase Castles in the Air, constructed by an obsession with self and adorned by a lust of self-glory. These intricate, city-like mirages continually change form, depending on the cravings of a soul who desires a Promised Land void of the Wealth of the Wait.

When we find ourselves forming "fairy" lands in our minds, envisioning our own kingship stage-center of the city, encapsulating God in the corners of our personal throne, we have committed witchcraft with the worship of the idol, Self. Fata Morgana leads to death, and only a gaze fixed on the cross will escape the seduction of a tantalizing demise.

"A hard worker has plenty of food, but a person who chases fantasies has no sense" (Proverbs 12.11 NLT).

* Mirage quotes found in Wikipedia.

Layers of Forgiveness

As God continues to align our understanding with His Word, our standard of what's normal will begin to change. The Holy Spirit hovers over the chaos of our lives, ready to transform us into the image of Jesus by implementing His eternal standard of holiness. When we allow God's Spirit full access into the innermost parts of our being, He will begin His work of dividing light from darkness—allowing us to fully abide in the goodness, favor and power of God's grace.

What was acceptable to us in days past will no longer feel right in our spirits. The Mind of Christ replaces our old nature (1 Corinthians 2.16), and we begin to transform from glory to glory into the image of Jesus (2 Corinthians 3.18). We now have peace in the midst of the storm. We claim authority over our enemies. We find abundance when the world sees lack. We walk in the path of blessings instead of curses. Every promise in God's Word is potentially ours as the Holy Spirit leads.

Forgiveness is essential in this process of sanctification (being set apart as holy). As we embrace and achieve this new standard of holiness, we will have to reconcile with people, experiences, behaviors and environments of our past. Our worldview and thought processes were shaped by the influences in our lives, and many of them were not aligned with God's Word and His standard of holiness. When our understanding is rooted in Christ, we will discover fresh hurt, disappoint, shame and guilt from that past that must be immediately released, so the enemy can't stake his claim there.

We will have to forgive people who didn't know better, circumstances that were out of our control and environments from our upbringing that were not godly. Most of all, however, we will have to seek forgiveness and grace for ourselves and receive healing, peace and comfort from the Holy Spirit. Our actions, behaviors and thoughts may have been committed in ignorance; but now that we have become aware of the discrepancies between our conduct and God's standard of right and wrong, we are accountable to confess, release and learn from those mistakes.

The enemy can only dwell in the darkness of our lives to which we give him access. God's light and mercy are more than enough to displace every ugly thing in our past, present and future. We have been made righteous (right-standing with God) through the covenant that Christ fulfilled on our behalf by taking our sins on the cross and pouring out His blood (life-giving essence) onto those who would receive salvation (2 Corinthians 5.21) (Ephesians 1.7). Because of Jesus we can stand blameless before a perfect God in bodies that have become beautiful temples for His Spirit (Colossians 1.21-22) (1 Corinthians 3.16-17).

So as we delve into a deeper relationship with Christ, we can eagerly embrace our new nature (2 Corinthians 5.17). But we must be ready to forgive! Forgiveness frees us from defeat and fortifies our faith.

"If we confess our sins, he is faithful and just and will forgive us our sins and purify us from all unrighteousness" (1 John 1.9 NIV).

Wandering Relativism

When I first moved back to my hometown seven years ago, I encountered a man in his mid-twenties sitting outside a local café. His clothes were a little unkempt, but nothing out of the ordinary for a young bachelor. He happily lounged in his chair, sipping his iced drink; and I thought there was something different about him, but I couldn't put my finger on it. All I knew was that he looked idle, like he had absolutely no agenda, no plans, no responsibility—nothing linking his thoughts to our external world. He simply took in and enjoyed the unfolding life around him.

I wondered if he might be homeless, but I quickly debunked the idea. He gave me a nod and a smile, and he seemed completely coherent in his interactions. He never asked me for money, and he didn't have the weathered worn appearance of someone living on the streets.

I've seen this man many times through the years—small glimpses of his morphing existence. A year ago, he came up to me outside a nearby grocery store. The jeans and t-shirt that once looked unkempt were now dirty and worn. He had lost much weight on his already lean frame. His fingernails were thick with grime and desperation had chiseled away his once serene expression.

He held out his hand to me and mumbled something about money. My heart instantly collapsed in disbelief, and I quickly opened my wallet to grab whatever I could find. I couldn't move as I watched him walk away. The idle man now lost.

Last week I saw him. He was walking along the feeder road of our highway as I drove to my destination. His skin was densely tanned, and his threadbare clothes drooped off his body. He was motioning with his hands and talking to himself. He wandered the streets in the labyrinth of his mind—no place in society, no purpose in God.

I don't know what experiences, decisions or actions have caused that man's feet to walk the path he has chosen. I feel nothing but compassion for him and wonder how God's heart aches for his beloved son. But I fear that society has fooled many people into believing that they are rooted in life and connected to purpose, but in reality they are wanderers, disconnected from absolute Truth, which is unchanging and eternal.

We live in the physical realm of our third dimension; however, our existence is merely a small glimpse of a reality tucked away in a greater, everlasting Kingdom. Our external world was given to us to teach us, prepare us and establish us in the spiritual Kingdom, but many people wander this earth in complete ignorance or denial of a spiritual reality. They have fastened themselves in the physical aspect of creation but stay blind to the Creator and His Eternal Kingdom.

What is worse, however, is that there are many Christians saved by grace but completely lost to their purpose in Christ. The origin of their straying is the spirit of relativism, and we have all been its victim. Relativism suggests that there is no absolute truth (which is already a contradiction because making a statement as truth about having no truth is incongruent). But the standard of relativism is not what trips us up. What causes us to stumble are the seeds of relativism hidden in our self-centered flesh, ego and pride.

God is truth (Deut. 32.4), Who expressed His truth in Jesus (John 14.6), in the Bible (John 17.17) and in the Holy Spirit (John 16.12-15). When we know His Truth, we are free from the endless work of our own pride (John 8.32). Our pride causes us to be submitted to relativism. We believe in God, but our opinions, actions and words change to protect our desires, our egos, our agendas, our comforts, our goals, our security and our glory. Our personal standard of truth becomes a baton that moves to the rhythm of our demands.

We bear the racket of our growing cacophony for a while, until we finally welcome any ruler—alcohol, pleasure, drugs, money, worry, security, lust, intellect, ignorance, approval, beauty—that drowns out the noise: a noise caused by our selfish lifestyle, completely disconnected from God and His Truth.

I've seen this wandering spirit in my own life. The changing levels of self-centered truth moving to suit my situation, my desires, my plans; until God finally confronted me with contradicting discord in my thoughts, words and actions. I've learned not to trust the desires of my own heart, until I have sought God's Truth (Proverbs 19.3).

I've also realized what God means about the absolute necessity of humility, as demonstrated when Jesus humbled Himself to give us freedom from our sins (Phil. 2.5-8).

When I stay subservient to real, lasting Truth, I will be humbled because I am a sinner, greased in grace, clinging to a perfect God; and I will endure the beautiful but painful metamorphosis of faith.

When Truth and I collide, I will be the one changing. I will be uncomfortable. I will struggle. I will be humbled. And I will be the one moving. But I will move in deeper wisdom and understanding because Truth is chiseling away at my pride and drawing me closer to God's eternal reality.

I don't want to be a wanderer in relativism. I want to be planted in Truth eternal. I don't want my words to mumble foolishness based on my sporadic, self-centered understanding. I want to speak coherent, unchanging words of Truth—no matter who is listening, no matter what the world thinks, no matter how I might look, no matter who gets offended, no matter the consequences— I will find my center in God and His expression of love to me through Jesus, the Bible and the Holy Spirit. I am freed from worry because my lips know only one language—the tongue of truth!

While the world wanders, I will remain in Christ.

"When Jesus spoke again to the people, he said, 'I am the light of the world. Whoever follows me will never walk in darkness, but will have the light of life'" (John 8.12 NIV).

The Bent Tree

I went to Moody Gardens in Galveston, Texas, with my family. One of the three pyramids in the Moody Gardens is a rainforest. We got to see many types of tropical plants, fish and animals; and my kids' eyes absorbed the new and exciting sights. Needless to say, I took a bunch of photos and even caught a monkey scaring a woman on video, which I gladly emailed to her.

The rainforest pyramid was filled with exotic foliage, and the shade provided by the drapes of green was nice in the mid-August heat. As we spiraled to the center of the rainforest, I noticed that the tip of the pyramid flooded with light, and directly below this apex trickled a beautiful man-made waterfall that flowed into a whirling rock-studded pond where birds lounged. Dense growths of trees surrounded this pond, but the cement area encasing the water prevented any plants from growing directly under the sunlight.

Tall palm trees outlined the cemented path, stretching high in order to capture some of the sun's rays funneled through the center of the pyramid. But I noticed one palm tree decided to find its light in a totally different way. Instead of growing straight up, it grew sideways for about 10-15 feet. Then once it made it to the clearing by the pond, it started growing up again toward the tip of the pyramid where sunlight poured in. This tree defied all odds, leaving the other trees to fight for the sun. It grew its trunk from the perimeter of the pyramid right into the center, and we had to walk around or duck under it in order to exit the rainforest.

I stared at the palm tree for several moments. It was about half as tall as the other trees, but it was more than likely longer than all of them. I knew its roots clung hard to the soil beneath it, so it could hold the weight of its horizontal growth. Although this tree had the same soil, root system and placement as the other palm trees, it grew bent for years to find its own light. This tree had a purpose beyond the crowd, and it chose a different path to find its destiny.

For many of us, the purpose growing in our lives is so different from where we started that God has to bend us, so we can reach our destiny. He doesn't want to give us new roots, because our families, backgrounds and experiences become the strength that makes us cling onto to Him. We want to grow straight up like everyone else; but, by no fault of our own, we have limitations that cause us to have great lack in the area God is calling us to. And the only way God can "straighten" our lives in agreement with His design is to break, bend and stretch us into the person we are to become.

But how stunning is the life that has been transformed by God! How strong the person who allows God's hand to change him and her! This person may not seem as "tall" as everyone else, but the distance he or she has grown can only be described as breathtaking. And when this person has exhausted all strength, energy and patience in years of reaching sideways, God will finally declare the time to grow straight up. This person will not hesitate. His or her eyes will be full of light (understanding) with resolution hard as diamonds and determination fueled for the race.

He or she will be wise as King David claiming the throne for his anointed family line, confident as Joseph telling the most powerful man alive how to save his country and zealous as Paul proclaiming the Good News to a world shrouded in darkness. He or she will be unstoppable, blazing a trail that will lead many to Christ. He or she will break away from the blinding vines of this world and transform into a unique masterpiece of God's design. And as everyone walks around the length of this person's extraordinary life, they will declare the creativity, power and the miraculous nature of our God.

"I will bring the blind by a way they did not know; I will lead them in paths they have not known. I will make darkness light before them, And crooked places straight. These things I will do for them, And not forsake them" (Isaiah 42.16 NKJV).

I Am Beloved

"Hang my locket around your neck, wear my ring on your finger. Love is invincible facing danger and death. Passion laughs at the terrors of hell. The fire of love stops at nothing—it sweeps everything before it. Floodwaters can't drown love, torrents of rain can't put it out. Love can't be bought, love can't be sold—it's not to be found in the marketplace" (Song of Solomon 8.6-8 MSG).

Reading Song of Solomon can bring a little blush to your cheeks. The intimacy, desire and passion found in this book of the Bible surpass any romantic effort that Hollywood pumps out. This beautiful work of God-breathed literature stands as the relational idea for marriage, but it also expresses God's love for His redeemed people, the Church. As I read Song of Solomon, I savored every word—reminding myself of God's intimacy, desire and passion for me. I enjoyed the romance until the Shulamite (The Perfect One or the Redeemed Church) can't find her Beloved (God). Her Beloved calls to her, but when she opens the door of her room, He is gone.

"I opened for my beloved, but my beloved had turned away and was gone" (Song of Solomon 5.6 NKJV).

The Shulamite instantly leaves her home and searches for her Beloved. She wanders the city streets, but the watchmen hit her and rip away her veil. She is wounded and vulnerable, yet she doesn't care. She is so desperate for her Beloved that she can think of nothing else.

"The watchmen who went about the city found me. They struck me, they wounded me; the keepers of the walls took my veil away from me. I charge you, O daughters of Jerusalem, if you find my beloved, that you tell him I am lovesick!" (Song of Solomon 5.7-8 NKJV).

I quickly began reading the rest of the text. I needed to know when and how the Shulamite finds her Beloved. More importantly, though, I wanted to know why the Beloved leaves her in the first place. There had to be a reason that He would call out her name, draw her away from the comforts of her home and lead her on a journey that would cause her to be physically abused, exposed and lost. In order to persevere as she seeks Him, the Shulamite continuously reminds herself of her Beloved's perfection and their intimacy together. Other people (the Daughters of Jerusalem) begin to notice her search, and they want to help her. After yearning for her Beloved, she ultimately discovers where He has gone!

"My beloved has gone to his garden, to the beds of spices, to feed his flock in the gardens, and to gather lilies. I am my beloved's, and my beloved is mine. He feeds his flock among the lilies" (Song of Solomon 6.2-3 NKJV).

The Beloved is in His garden! So the Shulamite woman wastes no time. She quickly makes her way to the garden. She has been through a lot to find her Beloved, and nothing will stop her from reuniting with Him. She is impassioned with determination and resolve.

"Before I was even aware, my soul made me like the chariots of *Amminadib*" (Song of Solomon 6.12 KJV).

The word Ammi means "people" and the word Nadib means "willing"; therefore, the Shulamite's soul is fierce as the chariots of "willing people"—ready and willing to do whatever it takes for her Beloved. Finally, an on-looker sees the Shulamite with her Beloved leaving the wilderness together!

"Who is this coming up from the wilderness, leaning upon her beloved?" (Song of Solomon 8.5 NKJV).

The Shulamite and her Beloved walk together, hand-in-hand, away from the wilderness and into the Beloved's garden where the fruit is ripe and plentiful and the King and His people are blessed from the harvest. And the Beloved whispers to His Bride, the Shulamite, that He longs to hear her voice in His garden.

"You who dwell in the gardens, the companions listen for your voice—LET ME HEAR IT!" (Song of Solomon 8.13 NKJV).

God gave me a simple explanation of why the Beloved had to leave the Shulamite: He had to draw her away from her self-centered comfort zone, strip her of her selfishness and self-reliance and lead her into His Garden where His abundance and presence dwell. And once the Shulamite is freed from all the trappings of this world, she walks in power and her voice rings aloud. She is no longer stuck in a man-made box of security; rather, she reigns free in the dominion and purpose granted her by the Most High God.

I remember the day that I started chasing God. He lured me away from my comfort zone with His promises and with His presence. I ran after Him like a child, not realizing that my journey would leave me lost, hurt and confused. I had to remind myself of the amazing beauty and perfection of my God. I had to cling onto the love He had for me, even though many times I thought that I couldn't feel it. I had to let go of all my hindrances and seek God with all of my heart. I became desperate to draw closer to Him and to find my footing in the center of His plan.

But I finally understand why I had to walk through the wilderness. I now see the beauty of being broken, exposed and reliant on a perfect and loving God. I've learned to lean on Him with my everything, as He brings me out of my selfish and aimless lifestyle. I trust Him even in pain and difficulty and know He will lead me to "His Garden" where my purpose fulfillment can bear fruit. I desire Him above all else, and I can say in confidence and with conviction, "I am my Beloved's, and my Beloved is mine!"

"Come, let us return to the Lord. He has torn us to pieces; now he will heal us. He has injured us; now he will bandage our wounds. In just a short time he will restore us, so that we may live in his presence. Oh, that we might know the Lord! Let us press on to know him. He will respond to us as surely as the arrival of dawn or the coming of rains in early spring" (Hosea 6.1-3 NLT).

Wasted on Judgment Day

"Remember that the Lord will reward each one of us for the good we do, whether he is slave or free'" (Ephesians 6.8 NLT).

God created a perfect world and a perfect people, which is symbolized in the Garden of Eden (presence of God or heaven) and Adam and Eve (humanity). But God gave us free will, which is symbolized in our free will choice to eat from the Tree of Knowledge of Good and Evil. Adam and Eve (humanity) chose to indulge in the tree's fruit (Genesis 3.6), which symbolizes evil (anything with the absence of Good or God), so now Adam and Eve's eyes were open to both Good and Evil and they lost their righteousness and saw their shame (Genesis 3.7).

Their sin creates a separation between them and God (death) because God is perfect and nothing imperfect can dwell with Him (Genesis 2.17). Adam and Eve had to leave the Garden of Eden (presence of God) and enter into the world where both good and evil dwell (Genesis 3.23 and Matthew 13.30).

However, God knew that we would use our free will to consume and create both good and evil, so He also put the Tree of Life in the Garden, which symbolizes Jesus—one of the three God-heads Who became human to wash clean the evil that humanity creates. (The other two God-heads of the Trinity are God the Creator Father and the Holy Spirit, the Counselor (Matthew 28.19)—three beautiful ways in which our God interacts with us.

Because of sin, Adam and Eve can no longer partake of the Tree of Life (Jesus) in the Garden of Eden (Heaven), so the Tree of Life clothes Himself in flesh, walks the earth and dies for our sins (Philippians 2.6-8). The Tree of Life comes to us!

Jesus died to redeem the effects of our free will; and in doing so, He erased every single evil (absence of God) we create in this world once we accept Jesus as our Savior and receive God's Holy Spirit (1 John 1.9). Jesus also perfects every single good (presence of God) we create, so they look like flawless gems to the Father.

We have only one chance—one life—to present Jesus with the flawless gems we produced with our free will once we get to heaven (presence of God). As Believers, we will not be judged by our sins (they are erased), but we will be rewarded for how we used the gifts and talents God gave us on earth.

By the grace of God, we have been given a foundation on Jesus Christ, but this foundation is only the beginning. God desires us to build something beautiful during our short time on this earth that glorifies Him. At the world's judgment in the final days, every person who has lived will be accountable to the "quality of each person's work" (1 Corinthians 3.13 NIV).

Our sins—laziness, pride, indifference, gluttony, selfishness, insecurity, fear, mistrust, lust, greed, malice, covetousness, worry, entitlement—will be void and clear, but what else will we have to show for our gift of life? The greatest tragedy for Christians will be to reach Judgment Day (Romans 14.10) and all their hard work on earth will be destroyed by death. Jesus' blood erased all their sins, but their eternal work rooted in obedience to the Holy Spirit is heartbreakingly small.

We must base our hard work on eternity because anything created to please this temporal world will be burned up by the fires of judgment. The enemy knows that he can't stop Christians from dwelling with God in Heaven once we die (John 10.28), so he will work his hardest to make sure we have nothing to show for our life here on earth. He will sedate us with pleasures, fill us with worries, tame us with fear, and try to focus our energy on self-glory—anything to prevent us from giving our free will over to the will of God. The enemy knows that if we are submitted to the Holy Spirit, our free will can be used for the purposes of God who will deposit our hard work in a heavenly vault with eternal rewards (Romans 2.6, Galatians 6.9 and 1 Corinthians 9.25).

I believe one of the biggest reasons Christians hold back from truly living for God is fear of making mistakes; but when we fear our mistakes, we lessen the all-encompassing power of the cross. Jesus' blood beautifies everything we create for the Father. The Father does not see our misshapen, discolored gems of good works we struggle to produce for Him out of obedience to the Holy Spirit; rather, He sees flawless, stunning gems that shine His glory to the world.

If we accept Jesus' sacrifice for our sins and ask Him into our hearts, the Father sees everything we produce through the lens of Jesus' righteousness and perfection. When we find ourselves before the Father, we can show Him our life's work of faith, and He will be well pleased to honor us with eternal rewards. Let's not waste a single moment!

"By the grace God has given me, I laid a foundation as a wise builder, and someone else is building on it. But each one should build with care. For no one can lay any foundation other than the one already laid, which is Jesus Christ. If anyone builds on this foundation using gold, silver, costly stones, wood, hay or straw, their work will be shown for what it is, because the Day will bring it to light. It will be revealed with fire, and the fire will test the quality of each person's work. If what has been built survives, the builder will receive a reward. If it is burned up, the builder will suffer loss but yet will be saved—even though only as one escaping through the flames" (1 Corinthians 3.10-15).

Squeezed Out

"Every branch in Me that does not bear fruit He takes away; and every branch that bears fruit He prunes, that it may bear more fruit" (John 15.2 NKJV).

For a special occasion, I got my hair done at a local hair salon. I enjoyed sitting back and letting the hairstylist wash and condition my hair. Then I read while she painstakingly blow dried and flat ironed my clean tresses to a beautiful, straight sheen. Since I live in a coastal town, the humidity loves to make my natural waves into a frizzy mess; so having smooth hair for several days without spending hours maintaining it was a nice treat.

I told the stylists that I rarely had time to style my hair. I explained that I had three small children, so it was difficult for me to invest the time it took to achieve the desired glossy locks. She asked me what I used to wash my hair, and I said I usually bought random shampoos and conditioners from the grocery store. She instantly went to the display items on the salon shelf and brought me two bottles. She told me that the shampoo and conditioner were anti-frizz formulated, and they would ensure my hair would be much sleeker and easier to style.

I said I would buy them without a second thought.

When I went to pay, I was surprised by the bill. I asked how much the shampoo and conditioner were; and when she told me, my eyes opened with shock. Although I never spent so much on hair products, I decided to make the splurge just this once to see if there was really a difference. I carefully carried out my designer shampoo and conditioner and brought them to my special shelf in the bathroom when I got home.

A few days later when I was ready to wash my hair, I accidentally squeezed out the conditioner in my hand thinking it was shampoo. Normally, I would have simply rinsed my hand in the water spray, but this conditioner was way too valuable for me to let run down the drain.

I took the top off the conditioner bottle and made sure to get every last drop of the precious anti-frizz formula back into its container. As I screwed the top back on, I had to laugh at myself. The value of the conditioner caused me to take great pains to use it well and not waste any of it.

God feels the same way about us. Through Jesus, God paid an unfathomable price for each of us, because He loves us and rejoices over us (Zephaniah 3.17). He has given each of us a valuable and unique purpose. He knows our presence on this earth is very short, so He wants to use us in precise and amazing ways. He doesn't want a single ounce of our destiny to be wasted on things that are not of Him and that have no eternal value.

Sometimes we feel like God is not working through us, but He is saving us for the perfect appointment at just the right time in just the right place. Other times we think God is bringing our movements into dead ends, but He is simply repositioning us back into our bottles of purpose, so He can apply us in better and more meaningful ways. God designed us to be a special formula for a specific need in His Kingdom, and we need to trust the Creator to direct our steps to their fullest and most effective path.

I want to be poured out with purpose. I don't want my time, energy and effectiveness to be wasted in the waters of indifference. I choose to live with meaning and use up all my resources to God's everlasting glory. I ask God that He will circumcise my heart and life, so I can be an instrument of His power, strength and love.

I pray that God cuts everything from my life that does not produce truth and that He squeezes every lost drop of Holy Spirit infused potential out of me until I draw my last breath.

"Circumcise yourselves to the Lord, And take away the foreskins of your hearts…." (Jeremiah 4.4 NKJV).

Stillness of Surrender

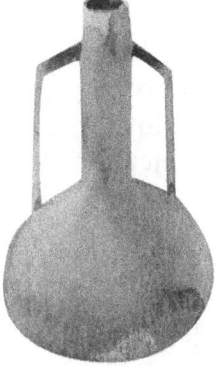

"The emptiness of an open heart creates a cavity for God to fill, but a closed mind never receives." - Bishop T.D. Jakes

I blinked and my pupils dilated in the dark. I jerked my head forward, banging my nose against the wall. I rolled onto my back and lifted my upper body with my elbows, trying to figure out where I was. I saw the outside light lining the shut door of my prayer room. I faced the door and followed the sunlit edge with my eyes, thinking back to God's promise:

"I know all the things you do, and I have opened a door for you that no one can close. You have little strength, yet you obeyed my word and did not deny me" (Revelation 3.8 NLT).

No matter what I do or how I feel that door has always been shut, and I had fallen asleep praying it open like a desperate king. A promised unfilled has made my heart sick, but my hope is fastened to the Tree of Life (Proverbs 13.12). I grasp a promise that I gain freely by grace, and I see a door that I claim opened by faith.

My Bible reading led me to King Hezekiah. His life was over; but as he lay in his bed dying, he leaned his face against the wall and prayed to God.

"Then he turned his face toward the wall, and prayed to the Lord, saying, 'Remember now, O Lord, I pray, how I have walked before You in truth and with a loyal heart, and have done what was good in Your sight.' And Hezekiah wept bitterly" (2 Kings 20.2-3 NKJV).

God pulled the shadow on the sundial back for Hezekiah and gave him 15 more years of life (2 Kings 20.10) (2 Kings 20.6). Hezekiah wrote a song, a declaration, of God's love and mercy: "The living, the living man, he shall praise You. As I do this day…." (Isaiah 38.19 NKJV).

The prophets are moved by the words of a king and write them down next to their own. And I wonder at Hezekiah's joy of receiving life that His song became part of the Word of God.

I didn't weep bitterly, I thought, as I got up and turned on the light. I sat down at my desk and reread the underlined verses in my Chronological Bible—2 Kings and Isaiah side-by-side. But I have wept bitterly over the years, and my mind replays my cries of disappointment and disillusionment; there are dozens of them.

I looked at my journal, eyeing the note I had scrawled before turning off the lights and lying on the ground, paralleling my body against the wall.

"I am not perfect. I will stumble and fall. Many people won't like or agree with me. I will say stupid things and make stupid decisions. BUT if I could simply remember to HUMBLE myself and give ALL glory to You, I will be okay."

I have fallen into a hole of humility, breaking my will to dust. I sit surrendered at the bottom, waiting for God to move. I am so empty of self that I feel vulnerable. But I need to be filled. I'm called a vessel, and I can't be hollow for long—something will fill me.

"Fill me, God!" I demand.

"Fill yourself," He says.

I'm so desperate for God's arm that I miss His correction. I yearn for the movement of His hand cutting away layers of indifference, denial, ignorance and sin. What more do I have to expose? I see the flaws of my humanity ever before me. I'm a sinner with a heart to please a perfect God. The pain of conviction seems better than this stillness of surrender.

"God, I am empty!" I command.

"Then take," He says.

What will I do with the emptiness?
What will I consume to fill my soul?
What will my stripped branches produce?
Where will my free will take me?

I will walk in the pleasure of the Lord.
I will fulfill the promises He has ordained.
I will make the Promised Land my home.
And I will enter heaven with confidence.

I won't face the wall with my prayer. I won't close the door and pour the oil. I won't hide in caves and sing the hymns. I won't preach in the wilderness to the crowds. I won't wear the lashes of Roman persecution.

But I will write my own story of salvation and wear my own scars of sanctification. I will take up my own cross of forbearance, and mark my own path of faith. And I will stretch out my arms and let Him slay me, so I can walk in His glory and reward.

"And hope does not put us to shame, because God's love has been poured out into our hearts through the Holy Spirit, who has been given to us" (Romans 5.5 NIV).

The Orange Bag

"Don't copy the behavior and customs of this world, but let God transform you into a new person by changing the way you think. Then you will learn to know God's will for you, which is good and pleasing and perfect" (Romans 12.2 NLT).

When I entered high school, I was a little different. I moved around with my family as an army brat, and I experienced different places, cultures and ideologies wherever I went. I started my freshman year with absolutely no idea of the local attitude or temperament of my new city and school. My naturally non-conformist behavior, speech and style caused my already threadbare self-worth to disintegrate.

During my sophomore year, I carried a small, bright orange 60s style bag as my backpack. I was the only one in school with this bag, and I'm sure I got a lot of looks. I didn't care, however, because I really liked the bag. I felt special to have discovered it. It went well with my long skirts and my hand-beaded jewelry.

I got a job when I turned sixteen as a waitress. I finally had my own money, and I remember my first purchase. I bought new leather boots that seemed to be popular around the school. Once I bought the boots, I started noticing the different brands of shirts and jeans that my classmates wore. Next, I bought a pair of jeans that were popular among girls.

The beginning of my junior year, I begged my parents for a name brand backpack that almost everyone in the school owned. I felt overjoyed when I put my books in that new backpack, and I gladly left the orange bag behind. I grew my hair long and styled it like other girls. And I began to act like the locals, incorporating their expressions, mannerisms and belief systems into my speech and behavior.

By my senior year, I blended in with the crowd perfectly. I remember walking down the hallway with my trendy shoes, jeans and backpack, realizing that I finally fit in. I smiled, feeling my self-worth (which was rooted in people-pleasing) bustle up with pride. I clothed myself with the expectations of others, and I felt secure in my conformity. Without knowing it, I had given up exceptional to be acceptable. At graduation, I talked with a fellow graduate who had remembered my orange bag, and he revealed that he had always considered it an awesome backpack.

Sadly, many times we Christians give up our unique purpose because we are so busy trying to be like everyone else. We grasp onto a certain design and forget that God has an awesome imagination that is able to create an infinite number of complementary expressions of His glory. God doesn't want us to fit in; He wants us to stand out. When people take notice, we have a ready audience to hear about salvation through Jesus.

The only way we can realize our full potential is by not analyzing what everyone else is doing. We can be excited for all that God is doing through others, while staying focused on what God is doing through us. God wouldn't waste a single life, and He has a unique design and purpose for each of us. We simply need to embrace our own symbolic orange bag and base all of our self-worth on God's unending love and hope for us.

"For we are God's masterpiece. He has created us anew in Christ Jesus, so we can do the good things he planned for us long ago" (Ephesians 2.10 NLT).

Tongue-tied

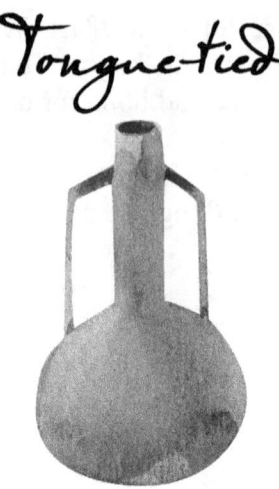

"It is the same with my word. I send it out, and it always produces fruit. It will accomplish all I want it to, and it will prosper everywhere I send it" (Isaiah 55.11 NLT).

Once a year a favored priest was selected to enter the Holy of Holies on the Day of Atonement. He prepared himself for seven days before entering the hallowed room of the temple. This was a once in a lifetime moment to be chosen as Israel's anointed mediator—an experience very few people could claim.

Zachariah was richly blessed with the privileged to enter in the Holy Place and stand before the presence of God. The other priests prayed from within the Temple and the crowd of worshippers confessed and offered praises outside the temple walls. The thoughts, attention and energy of all God's Chosen People were directed to God and the honored high priest on this holy day.

Not only had sanctified rituals made Zachariah's duties in the Holy of Holies exceptional on this special Day of Atonement, but an angel of the Lord appeared to Zachariah face-to-face. And not just any angel! This was Gabriel the angel who terrified Daniel with his very presence (Daniel 8.16), who explained the prophetic secrets of God's coming kingdom (Daniel 8.19-26) and who was delayed by the forces of evil 21 days when he was bringing a message to Daniel (Daniel 10.13).

There is 400 years between the Old and New Testament, which are called the silent years, and Zachariah is the beneficiary of God's first message to His New Testament people! The promise that Gabriel gives him sets the stage for the coming Messiah, the sacrifice and resurrection of Jesus, the age of the New Testament Church and the time of the Holy Spirit!

When most people exposed to God's glory fall flat on their faces with a deep awareness of their inadequacies, what does Zachariah do with God's message? He questions it! Gabriel reveals to Zachariah that God is giving him and his barren wife a son, but he is filled with disbelief: "Zechariah asked the angel, 'How can I be sure of this? I am an old man and my wife is well along in years'" (Luke 1.18 NIV).

And what does Gabriel do? He tongue-tied Zachariah, so he could no longer talk until his promised-child, John the Baptist, was born. "The angel said to him, 'I am Gabriel. I stand in the presence of God, and I have been sent to speak to you and to tell you this good news. And now you will be silent and not able to speak until the day this happens, because you did not believe my words, which will come true at their appointed time'" (Luke 1.19-20 NIV).

The power of the tongue speaks life and death, and if Zachariah couldn't speak life over His promise from God, then Gabriel acted in Zachariah's best interest when he silenced his mouth (Proverbs 18.21). Zachariah had become his own worst enemy. If it were not for Gabriel, Zachariah's tongue could have been the strongest force fighting against his God-given destiny, his eternal purpose and the happiness of his family.

This is a powerful truth for us today! When we question God, mistrust His leading and disbelieve His promises, we are actually fighting against our God-given destinies, our eternal purposes and the happiness of our families! If we can't decide to turn our disbelief into belief, our fear into faith and our death-giving words into life-giving words, we are better off silent.

So before we speak today, we must consider our words. Are we speaking life or death? Are we building up or tearing down? Are we giving God praises or complaints? Are we speaking God's Truth or the enemy's lies? We must learn to take captive every thought and submit it to God's authority, so we can claim God's promises and fulfill our God-given destinies.

"We demolish arguments and every pretension that sets itself up against the knowledge of God, and we take captive every thought to make it obedient to Christ" (2 Corinthians 10.5 NIV).

A Desperate Outlook

The first day of my senior year in high school, I realized that I didn't have lunch period with any of the few people with whom I had a close relationship. Two of my sisters and a handful of intimate friends who went to school with me all had the later lunch, and I was stuck at the early lunch surrounded by only acquaintances. Being an introvert and a senior in high school, the last thing I wanted to do was cultivate relationships with people I only knew in passing.

Although I had never gone to my guidance counselor out of my own initiative, I had no qualms about knocking on her door that day. I went straight to her office, sat down and cried in desperation. She had to find a way to switch my lunch period. There had to be something she could move in my schedule to reunite me with my sisters and friends.

She brought up my class schedule on her computer and compared my requirements with the classes available. She searched and manipulated every class arrangement, but she came up empty. There was simply no class that I needed that could fit into my schedule, which would leave the later lunch open for me.

She looked at me and waited for me to resign to the fact that I would be eating lunch alone my entire senior year, but I would not have it. I knew in my heart there had to be something she could do. I stared resolutely at her until she finally looked back down at her computer screen. I wasn't going to leave her office until I had a new printed schedule in my hand.

Tentatively, she asked me if I had taken honors Marine Biology. My counselor knew I didn't have the best grades. She had visited me several times regarding the fact that I couldn't pass Algebra 2. Also, I never took honors classes because I had very poor study skills. Luckily, however, my junior year, I decided to take one honors class because I thought the fun would outweigh the work. That class happened to be Marine Biology.

She looked pleased and somewhat shocked that I had taken an honors course. Then, she explained that I could be a teacher's assistant for Freshmen Biology.

"I'll do it!" I yelled.

Never in a million years did I ever think that I could be a teacher's aide, but my desperate situation caused me to look beyond my comfort zone and my standard of normalcy. At that moment, I was open to every and any possible solution to my problem. Through a very thin chance of likelihood, I obtained a wonderful role of responsibility that boosted my self-esteem and got me into the later lunch period.

Our experiences, personalities and understanding dictate the flow of our thoughts, choices and actions. We allow ourselves very few options in life because our imaginations are weak and our view of God limited. What we don't realize, though, is that God has infinite resources and a vast imagination, and His plan surpasses all comprehension. Oftentimes, He will allow our situations to become desperate, so we will be more willing to seek out alternate options and walk down unfamiliar paths.

When we find ourselves desperate and at a loss for a solution, we must stand firm in the promise that God is for us (Romans 8.31), and He will accomplish His promises to us (Romans 4.21). We can declare unwaveringly that God will provide a way through our roadblock, and then we need to look for God's unique supply to our lack.

As we learn to rely on the Holy Spirit's leading, our anticipation will begin to overshadow our desperation because we will trust that God will find a way when there isn't one. Our faith will increase every time we see God provide in powerful ways, and the excitement we gain from walking with the Lord will be hard to contain.

"For I am about to do something new. See, I have already begun! Do you not see it? I will make a pathway through the wilderness. I will create rivers in the dry wasteland" (Isaiah 43.19 NLT).

Faith Necklace

"He replied, 'Because you have so little faith. Truly I tell you, if you have faith as small as a mustard seed, you can say to this mountain, "Move from here to there," and it will move. Nothing will be impossible for you'" (Matthew 17.20 NIV).

A dear friend of mine gave me a faith necklace. The pendant strung on the slender rope of silver was a little glass jar with a single mustard seed in it. The gift was a beautiful symbol of Matthew 17.20, which contains Jesus' words about having faith of a mustard seed. I greatly valued this necklace because it came from my spiritual sister, and it became a rock of remembrance for me about my own faith journey.

Several months later, I wore the necklace to a family gathering. As I was talking to one of my nieces, I felt the Holy Spirit tell me to give it to her. I hesitated at first because the necklace was a gift, but I realized that my friend who gave it to me had paid forward countless possessions to others as the Holy Spirit directed. However, I also didn't want to give the necklace away because it was a tangible affirmation of my faith.

In the end, I surrendered to the Holy Spirit's leading. I had learned by now that God always blesses acts of faith, whether large or small, and His love is more valuable than the most priceless pieces of jewelry. I gave the necklace to my niece and explained to her that God wanted her to have it. Not only did she like the necklace, I believe the gesture poured greatly into her self-worth as a daughter of God. Through my obedience, God was able to show my niece a portion of His abounding love for her.

In the past, I would have researched this necklace and exhausted my time and energy trying to recoup what I had given away; but this time I placed the ball in God's court. If He wanted me to have my faith necklace back, He would have to provide it by His power and in His timing.

A few months later, I received a shipment of party supplies for my daughter's fourth birthday party. To my surprise, I found a package that did not belong with my order. I opened it up and in the plastic wrap were six brand new glass jar pendants, exactly like the one I had given away. I couldn't believe it! I quickly read the order to see what happened and discovered that the store was giving away a free gift from some of their surplus items. It seemed that they had enough jars to spare, and my little seed of faith had multiplied.

I was able to bless five other people with a faith necklace. In particular, I felt the Holy Spirit tell me to send one of them to my mentor who started a ministry in another town. She called me several days later weeping. Her faith had run low with many devastating blows to her ministry, and she needed God to affirm her faith steps. That night after she prayed, she opened her mailbox to find my faith necklace with a tiny faith seed in it. I explained in my note that I just wanted to thank her for always being such a faith warrior and godly role model to me.

I know this is a small example of God's amazing system of faith, but every time you make a sacrifice for God and His Kingdom, according to the prompting of the Holy Spirit, God will multiply it. The results may not be mailed to you directly, but they will materialize in real and exciting ways.

"Remember this: Whoever sows sparingly will also reap sparingly, and whoever sows generously will also reap generously. Each of you should give what you have decided in your heart to give, not reluctantly or under compulsion, for God loves a cheerful giver. And God is able to bless you abundantly, so that in all things at all times, having all that you need, you will abound in every good work" (2 Corinthians 9.6-8 NIV).

The Pride of Insecurity

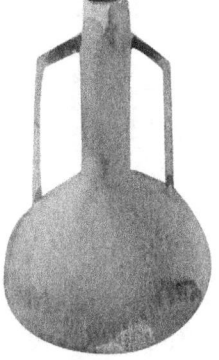

"Then Jesus came from Galilee to the Jordan to be baptized by John. But John tried to deter him, saying, "I need to be baptized by you, and do you come to me?" (Matthew 3.13-14 NIV).

I was talking with a friend who was asked to speak Sunday morning at a large church service about a topic for which she was extremely passionate. I asked her if she was nervous to go in front of all those people and talk.

She answered wisely, "It's not about me and how I feel. It's about what God wants."

Many times, Christians allow their own insecurity to stop them from obeying God's commands. What we don't realize is that insecurity is the negative form of pride. We are so self-focused and self-conscious that we have trouble seeing God and His will past our own self-centered insecurities.

Granted, it is difficult once we know God's perfection and our imperfection to humbly submit to some of the great things God calls us to. Many people in the Bible struggled with feeling unworthy to allow God to use them for His greater plan.

Moses didn't want to submit to God's call to set His people free because he wasn't eloquent (Exodus 4.10).

Gideon struggled to believe the angel when he called him a "mighty man of valor" (Judges 6.12-15).

Even Peter demanded that Jesus leave because Peter saw himself as a sinful man (Luke 5.8).

In the Gospel of Matthew, Jesus asks John the Baptist to baptize Him in the Jordan River. At first, John allows his insecurity to prevent Jesus from having His plan accomplished. He probably wonders how he could baptize Jesus when he isn't fit to untie His sandal (Luke 3.16). Jesus has to convince John to obey by explaining that His baptism "fulfills all righteousness" (Matthew 3.15).

Thankfully, John the Baptist gets over his self-focused worries and consents to Jesus' request! Can you imagine what would have happened if John the Baptist allowed his insecurity to prevent the fruition of God's plans for Jesus on this earth? It seems so shocking that John would "deter" the will of God, but Christians do this so often today.

We must realize that it's not about us. It's about what God wants. If God wants to use us in our imperfect state to accomplish His perfect will, who are we to stop Him? God wants His Children to play an important role in His Kingdom, and I marvel how it must grieve the Holy Spirit when we reject His plan because we are too focused on our weaknesses and not God's strength.

So I'm encouraged today to not allow my insecurity to prevent the fullness of God's purpose in my life. I'm determined to look past my flaws and the defects of my self-effort and grab tightly to the perfection of God and the redeeming work of Jesus on the cross.

"But he said to me, 'My grace is sufficient for you, for my power is made perfect in weakness.' Therefore I will boast all the more gladly about my weaknesses, so that Christ's power may rest on me" (2 Corinthians 12.9 NIV).

Speaking Face to Face

Moses is exhausted. He is the only person diligently seeking God in the entire, nomadic nation of Israel. He finally cries out to God, "I can't carry all these people by myself! The load is far too heavy! If this is how you intend to treat me, just go ahead and kill me. Do me a favor and spare me the misery!" (Numbers 11.14-15 NLT).

I smile when I read this because Moses' humility is so apparent. Many times pride steals our willingness to seek help. But not Moses—he was overwhelmed, and he let it be known. He was the single intercessor between God and the Chosen People, and he knew he had reached the end of his capabilities.

God does something amazing for Moses that demonstrates His divine grace. He takes some of His Spirit that He has placed on Moses and puts it on 70 Elders of Israel. It is obvious that these leaders didn't receive this Spirit by their own efforts. Two of the men who hadn't bothered to show up to the anointing meeting received the Spirit, as well. They disobeyed direct orders, yet God gave them His Spirit.

Moses' apprentice, Joshua, is at the anointing meeting, and he has never seen anybody but Moses prophesy (speak God's will) in the Spirit. He becomes very upset, and he pleads with his teacher, "Moses, my master, make them stop!" Joshua has been learning from Moses for a while, and I'm sure he feels jilted. How could these men receive for free what he has been working for all of his life? Joshua experiences first-hand the beauty of grace: a gift not based on the receiver, but on the Giver.

Moses' humility is displayed yet again when he looks at his young assistant and says, "Are you jealous for my sake? I wish all the Lord's people were prophets and that the Lord would put his Spirit upon them all!" (Numbers 11.29 NLT). Moses is a shadow of Jesus. Jesus is our intercessor, and God gives us His Spirit because of His love for us and the sacrifice that Jesus made for our mistakes. Jesus wants His sacrifice to spill God's anointing on every person. I'm sure Jesus repeats Moses' words, "I wish all the Lord's people were prophets and that the Lord would put his Spirit upon them all!"

A prophet is a person who hears from God, who sits with God, who sees God face to face and who communicates God's will. Yes, the gifting of prophecy can manifest in other ways, but the visions, dreams and riddles are merely outward signs of an inward discipline—seeking God. All Christians are called to sit with God, seek His will and tell others about His glory. At salvation we were each gifted with spiritual ears that hear God's voice. But are we using them?

Are we filling our lives with the world or with Him? If we want the fullness of God's Spirit moving in our lives, we have to make room for Him. If we want to discern His voice, we have to listen to and recognize it. If we want to tell the world about Christ, we have to seek Him every day and read His Word. We are honored with the power to communicate with God at any time. He is waiting for us. We just need to sit and talk with Him—face to face!

"And the Lord said to them, 'Now listen to what I say: If there were prophets among you, I, the Lord, would reveal myself in visions. I would speak to them in dreams. But not with my servant Moses. Of all my house, he is the one I trust. I speak to him face to face, clearly, and not in riddles! He sees the Lord as he is. So why were you not afraid to criticize my servant Moses?'" (Numbers 12.6-8 NLT).

Serving in Leadership

Solomon's son, King Rehoboam, lost half his kingdom (ministry) because he had no idea of the true meaning of leadership. He was at a crossroads, and he chose the wrong direction. His friends defined leadership as punishing people and forcing them to do his will. Yet the city elders knew the true core of leadership: "They said, 'If you will be a servant to this people, be considerate of their needs and respond with compassion, work things out with them, they'll end up doing anything for you'" (2 Chronicles 10.7 MSG).

Ministries are designed to provide for needs. As leaders, we are called to serve those around us. However, I think many of us get it wrong. Sometimes we serve to receive, we serve to grow our desires, we serve to be good enough, we serve to show others our works or we serve without the anointing of God. And we forget that serving becomes whitewashed unless we are doing it out of a pure heart to do God's will. God wants to cultivate a desire in us to serve the needs of others, but this desire does not come easily.

Our walk of service starts with those closest to us: spouses, children, siblings, parents and friends. We do not serve because we have to; we serve because that is our calling. We place our family's and friend's needs above our own, and work diligently to be Christ-like figures in their lives. Our family is our primary ministry, and we should be serving them first. They know everything about us, and they are the main witnesses to God's transforming power in our lives. I've come to the conclusion that if I am not fulfilling my husband's or children's needs, I have absolutely no right to be in ministry.

Once we find joy and purpose in serving our family, God will lead us to a small circle of people that He wants us to pour into and serve. This is not glamorous, and some people want to ignore it. But this is an important part of our own transformation. While we serve these hand-chosen people, God is able to do a good work within us. The fruits of our labor may not be outwardly obvious because the fruits are produced within us, building and strengthening our character and faith. Once God trusts us with leading our small group, He will begin to open doors for greater influence.

By now we are serving our families and others on a small scale, but our capacity (territory) is growing. God broadens our reach of influence now that we have strength to do more. However, this broadening may not look how we want it to look. We might be called to reach individuals, small groups or the masses; and they each have equal impact. The world's standard of success is different than God's, and we need to remember that He grows our ministries into the shape He has for them. We probably won't know the extent of our influence in God's kingdom until He shows us in heaven.

The critical aspect about having influence is that when we stumble, many people are affected. That is why during this entire process of learning leadership, God has been teaching us to rely solely on Him and to obediently serve Him. There is much Scripture on the accountability of leaders, and they shed light on the awesome responsibility of leadership.

Leading others through serving their needs is an amazing opportunity with a high cost. We must allow God to change our hearts if we are to lead effectively and righteously. I believe God would love for all His children to be shining-star leaders in our world today, but He will protect us from ourselves if we are not ready. We need to start with the basics and joyfully serve those we see every day. Only then can God securely position us on the path to doing more service for His kingdom.

"If anyone wants to provide leadership in the church, good! But there are preconditions: A leader must be well thought of, committed to his wife, cool and collected, accessible, and hospitable. He must know what he's talking about, not be over fond of wine, not pushy but gentle, not thin-skinned, not money-hungry. He must handle his own affairs well, attentive to his own children and having their respect. For if someone is unable to handle his own affairs, how can he take care of God's church? He must not be a new believer, lest the position go to his head and the Devil trip him up. Outsiders must think well of him, or else the Devil will figure out a way to lure him into his trap" (1 Timothy 3.1-7 MSG).

The Darkness of Faith

There are two types of darkness. The first one is where our enemy (Satan, Devil, Lucifer) dwells (2 Peter 2.4, Colossians 1.13, Jude 1.6). Any area of our lives that has not been exposed to God's light (Psalm 89.15, John 9.5, Job 33.28) is subject to Satan's influences because he has the ability to feed on the darkness that we hide.

"Satan has legal access, given to him by God, to dwell in the domain of darkness. Thus, we must grasp this point: The devil can traffic in any area of darkness, even the darkness that still exists in a Christian's heart." - Francis Frangipane: *The Three Battlegrounds*

The more of our lives we expose to God's light, the more the Holy Spirit can fully fill us: "The night is nearly over; the day is almost here. So let us put aside the deeds of darkness and put on the armor of light" (Romans 13.12 NIV). Satan has absolutely no authority in a mind and body completely submitted to God's light, so our honesty and humility is essential to achieving this "armor of light."

However, there is another type of darkness. This darkness surrounds our steps of faith and reveals our true intentions. God many times calls us into the dark, so we can behold His glory and all the good that it inhabits: "The people remained at a distance, while Moses approached the thick darkness where God was" (Exodus 20.21 NIV). It is in the darkness of faith that we demonstrate our complete trust in God and where He can pour out His abundance.

Four men with leprosy waited at the city gates of Samaria. The Kingdom of Syria had besieged Samaria, and the people were starving to the point of eating their own children (2 Kings 6.29). The four men couldn't go into the city because the people were destitute, yet they didn't want to continue waiting at the gate. Therefore, they decided to penetrate the darkness of the Syrian camp to beg for mercy (2 Kings 7.5). Once they got to the camp, they found it deserted, and they entered into the tents and obtained a great abundance.

"And when these lepers came to the outskirts of the camp, they went into one tent and ate and drank, and carried from it silver and gold and clothing, and went and hid them; then they came back and entered another tent, and carried some from there also, and went and hid it" (2 Kings 7.8 NKJV).

It is very difficult to walk into the darkness of faith. We have to let go of all our understanding and rely solely on the supernatural and eternal work of God. Sometimes we fear the direction God is calling us because we trust our sight more than God's voice (2 Corinthians 5.7). When we waver in our faith, we are exposing the reality that God is not the center of our lives. And when we elevate our understanding above God's, we miss out on the abundance that He has for us.

God is Creator and King of the universe, and only in Him can a life rich with purpose and abundance be found (John 10.10). The world is destitute, and we must not enter its gates to find our fulfillment. Just like the four lepers, we are all corrupted spiritually by sin; but if we cry out for mercy and take a leap of faith into the darkness, we will come face to face with a God who loves and cares for us. Only God can produce springs (blessings) in the desert places (emptiness, lack, hollowness) of our lives. So let go of your fear, and forge a new life of faith!

"I will make rivers flow on barren heights, and springs within the valleys. I will turn the desert into pools of water, and the parched ground into springs" (Isaiah 41.18 NIV).

Men Like Trees, Walking

Many scholars believe that Mark wrote down the words of Peter the Apostle to create the Book of Mark, the second Gospel in the New Testament: "The early Christian Fathers are unanimous in testifying that Mark wrote under Peter's superintendence by his authority. The 2nd-century Christian writer, Justin Martyr, goes as far as to name the Gospel of Mark 'Peter's memoirs'" (*The Preacher's Homiletic Commentary*, Mark, bk. 22, pg. 2-3).

So when we read Mark's account of Jesus' interactions with the disciples, we can understand that Peter's eyes were the receiver of the information and his mouth was the publisher. Mark listened to Peter and wrote down his words, so that we too could hear the revelations of Jesus and dig deep to find the treasures of Truth buried in them!

Only in the Gospel of Mark is told the story of the blind man being healed in the wilderness outside the small village of Bethsaida; therefore, something about this typical healing of a blind man spoke directly to Peter. In fact, it was after that account that Peter confesses to Jesus and the other disciples that "You are the Christ," a declaration Jesus "strictly charged them to tell no one" (Mark 8.27-30 NKJV).

"And they came to Bethsaida. And some people brought to him a blind man and begged him to touch him. And he took the blind man by the hand and led him out of the village, and when he had spit on his eyes and laid his hands on him, he asked him, 'Do you see anything?' And he looked up and said, 'I see people, but they look like trees, walking.' Then Jesus laid his hands on his eyes again; and he opened his eyes, his sight was restored, and he saw everything clearly. And he sent him to his home, saying, 'Do not even enter the village'" (Mark 8.22-26 ESV).

Peter has saved for us such a small story with such a profound revelation from God! Please explore a little of the history with me, so we can apply the truth to our lives today!

Bethsaida was in the region of Galilee. Included in Galilee was Nazareth, the village where Jesus was raised into adulthood. The people of both these villages show great unbelief and hardness toward Jesus as the Son of God. They had known Jesus' humanity, and they were incapable of seeing His divinity.

Jesus said about the people of Bethsaida, "What sorrow awaits you, Korazin and Bethsaida! For if the miracles I did in you had been done in wicked Tyre and Sidon, their people would have repented of their sins long ago..." (Luke 10.13 NLT). And Jesus said about Nazareth, "Truly I tell you," he continued, "no prophet is accepted in his hometown" (Luke 4.24 NIV).

Therefore, when the blind man was brought to Jesus, He led him into a desert place just beyond disbelieving people of the village. Incidentally, this wilderness is the same place where Jesus had just miraculously fed the 5,000 (Luke 9.10-22). Sometimes we must get away from the doubt of others in order for our faith to burst through.

Although it is not directly stated, we know that Jesus brought along His disciples with Him because the incident was recorded by Mark via Peter and because the blind man will prophetically see people who look like trees that are walking. Jesus purposefully brought His disciples into the middle of nowhere because He had something to show them.

Jesus does miracles and heals to prove His divinity, but He is always teaching the 12 individuals whom God entrusted to Him. They are His main mission because they will ignite the proclamation of salvation through Jesus' death on the cross to the world. Jesus prays to His Father with wisdom, knowing that His glory to the world would be displayed through the disciples:

> "I have revealed you to those [the disciples] whom you gave me out of the world. They were yours; you gave them to me and they have obeyed your word. Now they know that everything you have given me comes from you. For I gave them the words you gave me and they accepted them. They knew with certainty that I came from you, and they believed that you sent me. I pray for them. I am not praying for the world, but for those you have given me, for they are yours. All I have is yours, and all you have is mine. And glory has come to me through them" (John 17.6-10 NIV).

I'm sure the disciples were wondering why Jesus was wasting so much time, taking them all the way out to the wilderness to heal one blind man. Jesus had healed hundreds and hundreds of the blind, lame and broken. Why all this work for one man? It seems like such a low occasion compared to the high occasion of Jesus healing the "multitude" (Matthew 14.14).

I can see the disciples milling around the desert, waiting while

Jesus spat in this blind man's eyes, asking him what he saw. And what the man saw in the spirit before his eyes were "restored" was a message for the disciples, for the miracle benefited the blind man but the message benefited Jesus' most intimate followers. Only Peter stood close and still enough to hear it.

What did the blind man see? He says, "I see people, but they look like trees, walking."

As I contemplated this image, I knew that Jesus was whispering something to Peter, and this message reaches those of us who are willing to stay still and close enough to receive it.

Trees in both the Old and New Testament have a very profound meaning. They signify life-giving water is near. They provide shade. They bear fruit for eating. They produce material for establishing. If planted near a good water source, a tree can benefit many people. The fact that the blind man supernaturally sees the people around him (the disciples) as trees before his sight was restored makes for a beautiful picture of how God sees us.

The tree illustrates the righteous side of humanity. Our salvation is through the cross made of a tree. Jesus is the allegorical representation of the Tree of Life in Genesis and Revelation. Through the inspiration of the Holy Spirit written down in the Bible, God sees His people as trees.

"Blessed is the man who walks not in the counsel of the wicked, nor stands in the way of sinners, nor sits in the seat of scoffers; but his delight is in the law of the Lord, and on his law he meditates day and night. He is like a tree planted by streams of water that yields its fruit in its season, and its leaf does not wither. In all that he does, he prospers" (Psalm 1.1-3 ESV).

"To grant to those who mourn in Zion—to give them a beautiful headdress instead of ashes, the oil of gladness instead of mourning, the garment of praise instead of a faint spirit; that they may be called oaks of righteousness, the planting of the Lord, that he may be glorified" (Isaiah 61.3 ESV).

So what the blind man saw and Peter recounted was that God sees His disciples as amazing trees with the possibility to bear much fruit and provide God's children with the blessings of God's goodness. The only problem was that they were WALKING! They weren't planted fully in Jesus, the River of Life (John 7.38). They weren't still and close enough to receive from the Lord.

To be sure they were His most beloved disciples, but it would take the death and resurrection of Jesus for them to finally stop searching for meaning and purpose based on their own worth and works, and find their complete identification solely in Jesus! There is no life when we plant our roots outside of JESUS.

What a powerful message for us today! We are God's beautiful trees, but we need to stop walking and searching for meaning in other things. We can plant ourselves in money, feelings, our looks, pleasures, relationships, popularity, good works, personal strength or other fleeting idols. We can only find peace, rest, satisfaction and supernatural purpose when we stop walking and plant ourselves in Jesus. Only then will we become huge trees, full of fruit and a brilliant blessing to this world!

So let us be trees, planted firmly in Jesus Christ, so our roots can grow deep and our branches expand over the earth. And we can declare boldly like Peter that Jesus is indeed our "Living Hope."

"Praise be to the God and Father of our Lord Jesus Christ! In his great mercy, he has given us new birth into a living hope through the resurrection of Jesus Christ from the dead, and into an inheritance that can never perish, spoil or fade. This inheritance is kept in heaven for you, who through faith are shielded by God's power until the coming of the salvation that is ready to be revealed in the last time" (1 Peter 1.3-5 NIV).

Never Forsaken

The crucifixion is made up of three components, and physical pain is only one of them. Yes, Jesus is human, so the pain was a big part of why He said, "My soul is overwhelmed with sorrow to the point of death" (Mark 14.34 NIV). But I do not believe that it was fear of pain that made Jesus sweat drops of blood (Luke 22.44). I know that Jesus loves us more than we can comprehend, and He would boldly confront physical persecution for the sake of His brothers and sisters. I think He had a greater reason to feel anguish—a reason that our culture has trouble even understanding.

The second aspect of the crucifixion that may have caused Jesus to be filled with sorrow is that He became sin for us: "God made him who had no sin to be sin for us, so that in him we might become the righteousness of God" (2 Corinthians 5.21 NIV). Please note that Jesus became sin. He was sin for us. What is sin? Sin is the absence of God. Sin is the absence of light, love, beauty, glory, etc. Up to this point, Jesus had only eaten from the Tree of Life; He had never taken any fruit of The Tree of Knowledge of Good and Evil to His lips. His mind, heart and soul would be crammed by the culminated knowledge of the world's wickedness, produced by a people whose hearts were naturally sinful.

The third aspect of the crucifixion ties directly into the second. This was the "greater reason" that I was looking for. It took a while for me to comprehend, which demonstrates just how much I do not know about love. Several months ago, I was reading through the New Testament, and I was struck by the relationship between God and Jesus. They are so deeply rooted together, and I wanted to know how it felt. I prayed and asked God, "Show me how much Jesus loves You."

After I prayed that prayer, I read about Jesus praying to God in Gethsemane. His soul was in anguish, and God sent Jesus an angel to comfort Him. As I read about Jesus just minutes before He would be betrayed, I remembered how I had always been dissatisfied with explanations of the crucifixion. Yes, the physical pain Jesus endured was incomprehensible, but I know that there was another pain that I wasn't grasping. Finally, it hit me. If Jesus became sin, and God can have no part of sin, then God would have to forsake Jesus for a time.

Jesus loved God so much, and His entire existence was solely dependent on God; therefore, Jesus' biggest fear was to be forsaken by God. I believe Jesus feared this more than the physical pain and more than becoming sin. When Jesus cried out on the cross with His only complaint, He did not cry out, "My God, My God, this pain hurts so bad" or "My God, My God, this sin is so revolting." No, Jesus cried out, "My God, My God, why have You forsaken me?" (Mark 15.34 NIV). Nothing else mattered more to Jesus than the presence of God in His life. That is how much Jesus loved God. He loved God so much that He obeyed Him unto death. And this is the example I want to strive to embrace.

I know that God loves me no matter what, and I'm happy to say that I have forgiveness of my sins through Jesus. However, I want God to be my core. I want my relationship with Him to be the most important thing in my life—not just in my thoughts, but in my actions too. Jesus took my separation from God. He allowed Himself to be forsaken, so I wouldn't have to be. I don't want to take my relationship with God lightly. I can stand before the Father Who dwells in holiness only because Jesus paid the ultimate price: He allowed our sin to separate Him from His Holy Father.

Jesus is my Savior because of His complete obedience to God. Many times God asks me to do things that I don't want to do, but I do them out of obedience. I can trust, though, that God will never ask me to do it alone—God will never forsake me (Hebrews 13.5) and Jesus is always praying on my behalf (Romans 8.34). The words that Jesus whispered before becoming my Living Sacrifice have become my new life's prayer: "yet not my will, but yours be done" (Luke 22.42 NIV). Jesus died so I could live in eternity with God in heaven, and I will honor Him with a life of obedience. I may never be perfect, but I can be faithful!

A Ransomed Inheritance

"For you know that God paid a ransom to save you from the empty life your inherited from your ancestors. And the ransom paid was not mere gold or silver. It was the precious blood of Christ, the sinless, spotless Lamb of God" (1 Peter 1.18-19 NLT).

No matter how amazing our childhood and upbringing, we will always inherit a standard that is not aligned with God's Word. And no matter how horrible our childhood and upbringing, God is more than able to align us with His righteous standard. Through Jesus' work on the cross, every area of emptiness in our lives that we have inherited is made whole through the fullness of God (Colossians 2.10).

I believe the hardest sins to overcome are generational ones because the skewed reality they create has become our normal. God has His best path waiting for us and anything less is not good enough for His beloved children. However, if we don't realize that our lives are out of alignment with God's fullness and goodness, we will never seek adjustment.

Christ died not to give us an okay life. He died to give us an abundant life (John 10.10). We must believe it and reach out and claim it. The only problem is in order to have God's best, we must be willing to get vulnerable, let go and change.

Get Vulnerable: As humans, we are made up of both strengths and weaknesses. Pride tries to cover up our weaknesses and display only our strengths. Humility lays it all out on the line. No one is perfect. Sometimes we fear God's sting of judgment, so we hide our darkness from Him. The truth is, however, that it's our pride that stings. God's judgment for our sins fell on Christ; therefore, His holy conviction holds no sting of shame, and it directs us to a better way of life (1 Corinthians 15.56-57).

We can objectively look at our lives and ask God what ancestral heritage does not match up to His holy standard. Instead of allowing fear to cause us to hold these generational sins tighter, we can let them go with the awareness that we didn't ask for them, so we don't need to be embarrassed to get rid of them. Once we expose generational oppression in our lives, the Holy Spirit can do His work of removing them and replacing the chaos they cause with His peace.

Let Go: We are mere humans with very limited understanding of the workings of God's Kingdom, His plans and our purpose in this life. We cannot rely on our own strength, ability and knowledge to achieve God's best (Proverbs 3.5). God is good, loving and perfect; and He alone knows the paths of righteousness laid out for us (Psalm 23.3). We can confidently let go of all of our efforts apart from Christ, trusting that He has a better way.

There are areas of "normal" in our thoughts, beliefs and behaviors that may be way off from God's best. These faulty perceptions we inherited from our heritage enslave us to fear, guilt and defeat; yet Jesus has bought and paid in full the price for our freedom in His abundance, joy, peace and victory. It's time to shed any belief-system that does not speak the truth about us as defined by God's Word. God's Word says we are worth dying for (Romans 5.8), that we are children of God (Galatians 3.26) and that we have a purpose in Christ (2 Timothy 1.9).

Change: Once we perceive the lineage strongholds in our lives and let them go, the Holy Spirit will begin His work of transforming us into the image of Christ (2 Corinthians 3.18). Now starts are "new normal" that usually doesn't feel comfortable at first. Like anything new, we must walk in our discomfort until God's truth becomes our holy standard. The Bible says we are more than conquerors in Christ (Romans 8.37), that we are God's royal priests (1 Peter 2.9), that we are the righteousness of God through Jesus Christ (2 Corinthians 5.21), and that we have everything we need to live a godly life (2 Peter 1.3).

The beautiful promises given to us by God will feel out of place according to the world's standard, but we must believe these truths if we are going to claim them. All transformation takes work. There is a work of shedding the old and embracing the new, allowing the core person God formed in us to shine forth (Ephesians 4.22-24). We are God's masterpiece, and His designs are always valuable, unique and lovely (Ephesians 2.10).

Once we become vulnerable to Him, let go of our "normal" and allow the Holy Spirit to change us, we will walk forth a new creation in Christ.

"This means that anyone who belongs to Christ has become a new person. The old life is gone; a new life has begun!" (2 Corinthians 5.17 NLT).

Hagar's Wellspring

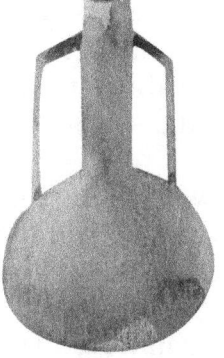

Abraham sends Hagar away along with their son. Abraham is extremely wealthy and obviously cares for his firstborn son because he is very displeased when his wife, Sarah, demands that he send them away (for they will not share in Isaac's inheritance); however, God tells Abraham to do as his wife says (Genesis 21.12).

What is surprising is how little Abraham is allowed to give Hagar and his son for their journey. The Bible reads that Abraham took "bread and a skin of water and gave it to Hagar, putting it on her shoulder, along with the child, and sent her away. And she departed and wandered in the wilderness of Beersheba" (Genesis 21.14 ESV).

Abraham gives Hagar some bread and a single skin of water. This meager supply of resources doesn't even get the son and mom duo across the wilderness. And notice everything was put on Hagar's shoulders. She has to bear the burden of trying to survive with no one to help her.

Hagar comes to the end of herself and places her son down to die. Even though she sits a distance away, she never leaves him. She has carried her promise as far as she humanly can. Though all seems lost and death is imminent, she does not try to save herself by abandoning her son. It is interesting to note that when Hagar cries out, God is recorded to hearing the voice of the boy and not hers (Genesis 21.17). It was God's promise to Hagar that moved Him, not the effort she put forth.

Finally, Hagar is included with the Patriarchs and receives a blessing for her son and offspring: "Up! Lift up the boy, and hold him fast with your hand, for I will make him into a great nation" (Genesis 21.18 ESV). Hagar opens her eyes and before her is a wellspring, and she takes her withered, dried skin and fills it with water and gives it to her son. God beautifully transforms desolation into abundance.

Gleaned Truths

1. The world will not give us the full resources we need to see our promise fulfilled.

2. God will bring us to the end of our resources before He blesses us with His abundance.

3. The test is not whether we work hard enough for our promise. The test is whether we will not abandon our promise in the wilderness.

4. God fulfills His promises to us not because of our faithfulness but because of His faithfulness to His promises. All of our efforts fall short of God's glory, so He relies on His perfection, extending love, mercy and grace to us.

5. God will provide a wellspring of life in the middle of our wilderness if we do not give up.

6. God loves to make something out of nothing in order to magnify His love, glory and faithfulness in our lives as a demonstration to an unbelieving world.

7. We must not rely on our strength or the strength of others. Only God's mighty hand can redeem our promises and bring them to pass against all odds.

"Then God opened her eyes, and she saw a well of water. And she went and filled the skin with water and gave the boy a drink" (Genesis 21.19 ESV).

Jesus in the Details

My husband and I took our family to our mentor's ranch for the first part of our Thanksgiving vacation. Yesterday, as my kids played with the goats, dogs, chickens and other animals, their shoes became muddy.

When I saw the mud-caked shoes, I knew right away that I would be cleaning them that night. My mind sees these small details, and though they seem minuscule to some, I know how important the small details are to the larger picture.

As I smacked the shoes together, grassed mixed mud flying every which way, I had to smile. Jesus had already prepared to show up in this detail of my life before it even happened. That morning I flipped my Bible to the Book of Luke. I read how a group of women, including Mary Magdalene, Joanna and Mary, the mother of James, had found Jesus in the small details of life.

The women noticed that Jesus' body wasn't cleaned properly for burial, and they prepared to take care of that detail—a detail that may have been lost in the light of the bigger picture of our Savior's death. Others overlooked this detail, but not the women, and Jesus showed Himself mightily in it.

"And the women who had come with Him from Galilee followed after, and they observed the tomb and how His body was laid. Then they returned and prepared spices and fragrant oils. And they rested on the Sabbath according to the commandment" (Luke 23.55-56 NKJV).

They had observed the detail of Jesus' body, and they knew right away that they would be taking care of it.

After I got the thick mud off my kids' shoes, I walked over to the barn where the water hose was located. I sprayed the shoes gently with water, rubbing the dirt off with my hands. I thought of the women going to the tomb, determined to take care of the detail of Jesus' body. How would they move the rock that covered the tomb? Their thoughts were on the details, so God would have to take care of the big picture.

But Jesus' body wasn't there. Another woman had already taken care of the detail, anointing His body with expensive oil for his burial. The disciples had complained because they thought the money was being wasted. They didn't realize Jesus would be dying soon, but Jesus knew God was preparing His body for death. God was already in the details, and the woman who responded to God's call would be remembered for eternity.

"For in pouring this fragrant oil on My body, she did it for My burial. Assuredly, I say to you, wherever this gospel is preached in the whole world, what this woman has done will also be told as a memorial to her" (Matthew 26.12-13 NKJV).

Instead of cleaning Jesus' body, the women who gathered to respond to the detail got to experience the first proclamation of His resurrection. The angels appeared to them and exclaimed that

He had risen! The women ran in their excitement, joy and awe, and they were the first to tell the world about the Good News: JESUS IS ALIVE!

"And it happened, as they were greatly perplexed about this, that behold, two men stood by them in shining garments. Then, as they were afraid and bowed their faces to the earth, they said to them, 'Why do you seek the living among the dead? He is not here, but is risen! Remember how He spoke to you when He was still in Galilee, saying, "The Son of Man must be delivered into the hands of sinful men, and be crucified, and the third day rise again""" (Luke 24.4-7 NKJV).

I finally put my kids' shoes on a tree stump to dry. I had accomplished the detail set before me. My kids would be able to run and play another day in their shoes. But more importantly, Jesus showed up powerfully in the details of my life. There is nothing too small that He does not notice. In fact, I think Jesus likes to show off in the details of life because a serving heart can be found there. The women at Jesus' tomb found Jesus in the details, and so did I.

As we focus on serving others with the small details that make up our day, we can joyfully thank Jesus for being with us. He can be found in every detail of our lives, and in each moment, we can proclaim the Good News that JESUS IS ALIVE!

I value all the small details that God gives me because I know they make up the fullness of His movements in my life. Jesus calls me to clean my family's muddy shoes and to write words for His glory. He notices both details equally!

"The Lord directs the steps of the godly. He delights in every detail of their lives" (Psalm 37.23 NLT).

Garbage Out

There were two trees in the Garden of Eden: Tree of Life and the Tree of Knowledge of Good and Evil. God warned Adam and Eve not to eat from the Tree of Knowledge, but the snake tempted them to eat fruit from this tree. They did, and their eyes were opened to their nakedness.

We all know this story, and we pity Adam and Eve for eating the forbidden apple, yet we consume poisonous apples daily and think nothing of it.

Tree of Knowledge is the symbol of our free will to consume evil. The snake is the symbol of the fallen Arch Angle Lucifer (Satan) who before his fall was called "the star of the morning, son of dawn" (Isaiah 14.12). The fruit is the symbol of the fruits of evil. Adam and Eve's consumption of the fruit is the symbol of sin. Sin separates us from God. God is all-good. Something that is 100% genuine cannot mix with any other elements. God is 100% good; therefore, everything that has the absence of good (evil, sin, darkness) cannot mix with Him. Those things are un-God. There is no in between. God did not create evil, but since He created good, the absence of good exists.

God gave Adam and Eve free will and they chose to allow evil to enter into a creation that was made very good by God (Genesis 1.31). They consumed sin with Satan, and this sin corrupted God's beautiful design. Because of God's mercy and love, He came down to this corrupted earth and became a man we know as Jesus. Jesus felt the full repercussions of sin—He felt pain, hunger, temptations and death; yet, He lived a blameless life. Our 100% perfect God came into our 100% corrupted world to show that He could still live a 100% blameless life. He consumed no apples while He walked among us, yet He tasted the fullness of their poison. He took that poison within His body, so that whenever we take bites of our apples, He pays the price.

There are fruits of evil all around us, and we daily have the choice to consume them. These fruits are on TV shows, movies, music, books, Internet, conversations, relationships, actions, thoughts, attitudes, etc. I'm not going to go into the specifics of what is evil and what is not. If you are a Christian, you have the Spirit of God residing in you. If you are daily allowing the Holy Spirit to guide you, He will tell you what is good and what is evil. You'll feel it in your soul (Galatians 5.16-25).

Our culture today relishes in pushing the boundaries of the knowledge of evil. Every aspect of media and day-to-day life dives into the unexplored knowledge that seems beautiful, delicious, new and interesting. It all appears exciting at first: a provocative new love affair, a sophisticated act of mayhem, a piercing insight of torture, a hilarious act of perversion, a subtle twist of purity. And we fill our hearts and minds with it. Christians are consuming sin by the fistful, and we think that we are doing nothing wrong. We act like we have it all together; but when disaster hits, our true colors show. Many Christians are depressed, defeated and distraught. We have forgotten that what goes in, must come out.

I'm not saying that you won't experience hardships because you will. Jesus lived a blameless life, but He experienced the effects of sin because the world is corrupted. Yet, with our choices we can tip the scales towards blessings or towards curses. Before the Israelites entered the Promised Land, God told them that they can choose a life of blessings or curses (Deuteronomy 30.15-16). God said specifically that the path to blessings was not hard to achieve: "Now what I'm commanding you today is not too difficult for you or beyond your reach" (Deuteronomy 30.11 NIV). How do we achieve the path of blessings vs. the path of curses?

Here is a simple formula:

Consuming fruits of sin from the Tree of Knowledge of Evil = a path of curses.

Consuming fruits of God from the Tree of Life = a path of blessings.

God told the prophet Ezekiel to eat the scrolls (Ezekiel 3.3). King David meditated (ponder and contemplated) on God's laws because they were like honey (Psalm 19.9-10). Jesus broke the bread and said, "Take it; this is my body" (Mark 14.22 NIV). God's Word, God's Commands and God's Son are all fruits from the Tree of Life. What I fear for myself and for other Christians is that our daily intake of fruit is 99% from the Tree of Knowledge and only 1% from the Tree of Life. God has tested me on this, and I failed miserably (Psalm 26.2); but I'm determined to do better!

God makes a promise to us. He said that if we consume from the Tree of Life, we shall be blessed. My prayer is that Christians (me included) would drop all the apples and start clinging to

God's Word. Satan was once the bearer of light, and he can make sin seem beautiful. The beauty of sin is rooted so deeply in our lives that it's hard to see it; and the only way we'll ever be able to distinguish it is if we explore the opposite—God! When we start cultivating a deeper, more meaningful relationship with God, all those apples that seemed acceptable at first start to repulse us. Once we experience the holiness of God, the ugliness of sin becomes extremely apparent.

The world has made the Tree of Knowledge seem so exciting and awesome, but the fact is that nothing surpasses the power and glory of the Tree of Life! It is up to Christians to choose the path of blessings and show the world how totally amazing our God is! I know that the apples in your life may seem to taste good and look trendy, but I promise you that if you sacrifice them for God and replace them with fruits from the Tree of Life, you will be blessed. I can make such a bold promise because God promises it in His Word.

I love Christians who make an effort to set themselves apart from the world, yet maintain a high regard in the world's eyes. I can think of several Christian—athletes, singers, movie stars, scientist, entrepreneurs and writers—who are admired by Christians and non-Christians alike. In the New Testament when the church was in its early stages, the Bible says that many people admired the church members, though they didn't join the church (Acts 5.12-14). Not everyone is going to become a Christian and not everyone is going to agree with our faith, but we still should be admired for our integrity, our work ethic, our selflessness, our compassion, our talents and our love for others. We still should lead lives worth emulating. That is why it is so important to eat from the Tree of Life!

I want to assert again that God cannot create evil. Lucifer was created as the most beautiful angel ever—Lucifer means light-bearer. When God created Lucifer, the absence of Lucifer was also created. Everything has its opposite because of its absence; it's what defines it. Because Lucifer fell away from God, he became the opposite of the light-bearer. He became the bearer of darkness (Ephesians 6.12). Evil was created because of our free will to eat fruit of the Tree of Knowledge.

We can embrace God (God is all-good, all-love, all-holy) or we can embrace un-God (evil, hate, corruption). God gave us the choice; otherwise, we would just be robots. When we embrace God and accept Jesus as a payment for our wrong choices, we go to heaven (the place that has God). When we shun God and do not accept Jesus as payment for our wrong choices, we go to hell (the place that does not have God). Everything that is evil is merely the absence of what God made. We decide which direction we go—to God or away from God.

I know you might wonder why God created anything in the first place because everything He creates has an opposite. However, when I look at my life, my husband and my children, I feel so much love and good. I'm glad God created us. God created a family. He didn't have to, but He did. I rejoice that He did. I would rather be confronted with the Tree of Knowledge than never exist at all. So guard yourselves, my friends. Guard yourselves from the Tree of Knowledge of evil.

"He who has an ear, let him hear what the Spirit says to the churches. To the one who conquers I will grant to eat of the tree of life, which is in the paradise of God" (Revelation 2.7 ESV).

Kingdom Faith

I would like to stress that the word "kingdom" denotes a King—the King, the Creator, our God. In order to have the fulfillment of God's Kingdom (His purpose) in our lives, we need to first have a relationship with the King. The only way we can have a relationship with the King is through His Son, Jesus. Once we have a relationship with Jesus, we receive God's Spirit (Holy Spirit) to guide us. God, Jesus and the Holy Spirit are three separate components of God, but they are all God.

Jesus' life was foretold by the prophets (Isaiah 53.3-5) in the Old Testament and was fulfilled and documented in the New Testament (Matthew 27, Mark 15, Luke 23 and John 19). During His ministry on earth, Jesus taught us to "Repent, for the kingdom of heaven is near" (Matthew 4.17 NIV). There is an overall Kingdom fulfillment for this world that Jesus foreshadows in Luke 21; however, I believe that God has planted in each of us a Kingdom fulfillment.

I find it interesting that Jesus compared the Kingdom of Heaven to yeast. Yeast is dormant until it is placed in bread dough. (I believe that each of us has a Kingdom fulfillment, yet it will stay dormant until we accept Jesus as our Lord and Savior.) The yeast works on individual particles in the dough and transforms them. The end result is a sweet, yummy loaf of bread (John 6.51).

This Kingdom image leads me to believe that we all have a kingdom purpose to fulfill, which will be a part of the Kingdom purpose of all existence. God's Kingdom fulfillment has already been established. His Kingdom will come whether we participate or not. It will be a shame, though, to see Jesus coming down from the skies riding a flying horse and realizing that we snoozed through this life and never fulfilled our purpose (Revelation 19.11).

Humans have two parts: We are flesh and spirit. Genesis 2.7 explains that "the LORD God formed the man from the dust [flesh] of the ground and breathed into his nostrils the breath of life [Spirit], and the man became a living being" (NIV). When we ask Jesus into our hearts, God plants His Kingdom purpose into our spirits. The only way we can fulfill our purpose is if we live in the spirit. The problem is that it is so much easier to live in the flesh. To live in the spirit takes A LOT of faith. The flesh and the spirit are always struggling for dominion. A person cannot live divided. Either she or he is walking in the spirit or in the flesh. There is no middle ground.

So what do we do? How can we ensure we live in the spirit, so that we can fulfill our Kingdom purpose? The answer is easy, but it may not seem pleasing at first...hardships.

God allows hardships in our lives for two main reasons: First, they kill our flesh. As Christians, we need to desire the death of our flesh because, otherwise, we will never fulfill our Kingdom purpose. Since our flesh and spirit are constantly warring for control, God does us an absolute favor when He sends hardships our way to take out the flesh (Galatians 5.24, Romans 6.2,

Romans 8.13). We will always be drawn to live in the flesh because it is just easier. If we allow God to beat down our flesh, we will more likely embrace the spirit.

Second, hardships build our faith. Faith is the key. According to our faith will our Kingdom purpose be done (Matthew 17.20). It is interesting that we embrace physical exercise because we know it's going to build our bodies, yet we don't embrace hardships, which will build our faith. Every time we endure hardships and continue to believe God for His promises to us, our faith becomes stronger. We must have stellar faith in order to live in the spirit.

Faith is essential to fulfilling our Kingdom purpose. God is going to do something in us that will go against all odds (Matthew 19.26). We will need lots of faith to believe that He will work His beautiful plan through our messed-up lives (Philippians 1.6). The surest way to build faith is through hardships. Hardships come in many forms, but we can claim victory to overcome them through Jesus Christ (1 John 5.3-5). When the sin of this world increases, God's grace increases (Romans 5.20). And we can do all things through Christ (Philippians 4.13).

I'm determined not to give-up when hardships come my way because I know that when my flesh is weak, my spirit will become strong (2 Corinthians 12.10). There is a battle between my flesh and spirit, and I want my spirit to win. It is only when we go through hardships, we can ensure that we fulfill the Kingdom purpose God has for us: "where they strengthened the believers. They encouraged them to continue in the faith, reminding them that we must suffer many hardships to enter the Kingdom of God" (Acts 14.22 NLT).

Therefore, let us face our hardships with determined victory because they bring to completion God's Kingdom fulfillment in our lives: "But rejoice that you participate in the sufferings of Christ, so that you may be overjoyed when his glory is revealed" (1 Peter 4.13 NIV) and "Now if we are children, then we are heirs—heirs of God and co-heirs with Christ, if indeed we share in his sufferings in order that we may also share in his glory" (Romans 8.17 NIV).

Faith Words on Writing

A Writer's Grace

Many times after I write a post based on an insight that the Holy Spirit has given me, people will mention another aspect of the insight that I didn't explore. Or I read posts that describe beautiful, God-given insights, and I will discover a different angle based on their research. It seems that no matter what I read or write, there is always more to it.

People who write about godly insights offer up their efforts only to realize that they've come up short. We will never be able to describe the fullness of every God-given insight. There will always be a different angle, a different aspect, a different interpretation, a different application and a different relevancy. This realization can cause writers to shirk back or give up. Why would we continue writing on matters that we will never be able to fully explain? Why do we willingly risk getting attacked, condemned, criticized and humiliated?

I've come to a few conclusions that help me claim Writers' Grace.

First, the Word of God is living: "For the word of God is living and active. Sharper than any double-edged sword, it penetrates even to dividing soul and spirit, joints and marrow; it judges the thoughts and attitudes of the heart" (Hebrews 4.12 NIV).

God's Word doesn't change, but I believe that it is organic like a beautiful tree. Its roots run deep, its branches stretch wide, its limbs reach high, each leaf is unique and each fruit tastes different! Therefore, when I describe a God-given insight, I'm only able to write about what I could capture. The tree is too much, too powerful, too awe-inspiring for me to do it justice, but I can explain the little bit that the Holy Spirit has given me.

I love the book of Job, especially in chapters 40 and 41 when God finally speaks up after remaining silent for so long. God gives Job a glimpse of His magnitude, and Job is overwhelmed. Job replies, "...Surely I spoke of things I did not understand, things too wonderful for me to know" (Job 42.3 NIV). Even Job who was "blameless and upright," felt inadequate to understand the works of God (Job 1.1 NIV). I've decided not to worry about having the fullness of God's knowledge because it's not possible. I just want to make sure that I get all the insights that God has prepared for me.

Second, if we knew everything we wouldn't need God. God gives us tidbits of His yummy insights as we draw near to Him. The more we eat of God's Tree of Life, the more we crave it. Yet we will never be able to consume the entire Tree. So every Christian writer needs to wave a white flag and admit that she doesn't know everything and she never will. Also, we need to give each other some "plate room." We look at another Christian's plate and complain that he is consuming different fruit than we are, so somehow his spiritual food is wrong. However, many times the fruit on his plate was plucked from the same branch that we got ours from.

Third, our lack of understanding keeps us reliant on others. It's easy to feel super-spiritual when we are by ourselves; though, once we are around people for a while, it becomes painfully obvious that we still have a lot of growing to do. God wants us to learn from each other; otherwise, He would have ended the commandment at "Love the Lord your God" and not have added "'Love your neighbor as yourself" (Matthew 22.37-39 NIV).

I imagine Christians who seek godly insights as collectors of the Tree of Life. They each have their arms loaded with different leaves, fruits, bark and soil. When I learn from them, I acquire all the treasures that they have found. I enlarge my image of the Tree. As long as their treasures come from the Source, who am I to judge if their leaves come from a different part of the tree than mine? In fact, the broader my collection spans, the better understanding I will have of the Tree's greatness.

I love the story found in Mark about the disciples who ran to Jesus to tattle tale on an unknown man driving out demons in Jesus' name. Jesus' reply was interesting: "'Do not stop him,' Jesus said. 'No one who does a miracle in my name can in the next moment say anything bad about me, for whoever is not against us is for us'" (Mark 9.39-40 NIV).

This story is where I found my Writers' Grace. If we, as writers, are driving out the enemy in people's lives and bringing them closer to Jesus, we are on the right track. If we are sitting with God and gaining His insights, it doesn't matter what side of the tree they come from. No single person can know the breadth and depth of God's knowledge. No single person will have the end-all to one insight. What a relief!

So before we go criticizing others who are willing to expose themselves as fools for God, we need to ask ourselves this: "Is this insight rooted in the Tree of Life? Does this insight point to Jesus? Are people being drawn to Jesus because of this insight?" We can apply this same standard to individuals, churches, ministries, etc. They might not be a part of our little circle of influence, but they could be a part of God's unending circle of influence.

Obedient Mistakes

After reading, editing and printing out each devotional for my first writers' group, I thought everything was nearly perfect. We were half way done with putting all of the devotionals together, when I noticed it: A big fat error on one of the devotionals, specifically, my devotional. It was an error of information, which I had researched and wrote down incorrectly. It was blatantly wrong and staring at me in the face. I was so upset at myself and God. Why would God allow me to make a mistake? Why would He have me start something when He knew that I would mess it up?

I was very critical of my published work, and I knew there would be people out there just like me who would notice every mistake. I went straight to the computer and fixed my mistake. Then I printed out two hundred copies of the new page, dismantled all of the devotionals and started to replace the wrong page with the corrected page. I was halfway done again when I noticed a formatting error on the new page that was inconsistent with the rest of the book. I became even angrier.

Here I was wasting my time, replacing one mistake for another.

Why had God allowed me to make another mistake? It felt like He was doing it on purpose. Now I needed to correct the new mistake, print out two hundred more copies, dismantle all of the books again and fix everything. I wanted to scream.

As I hurried down the hallway in my house, I felt God telling me to pray. "Fine," I yelled and fell to my knees on the carpet. God immediately said, "You will make mistakes. You are not perfect, but that will not stop Me from receiving glory from your work. It will not stop my perfect will from being done."

I realized it then. I will not be able to produce anything perfect, but that should not deter me from doing God's will. He will cover my mistakes with His grace, and His perfection will be seen through my imperfections. What a relief! I can make mistakes! And I am determined that from now on, I will not be so critical of other people's mistakes. Mistakes don't matter if they are done in obedience. We can see past the errors of human effort and focus on the faithfulness of God's perfect plan.

"Great peace have they who love your law, and nothing can make them stumble" (Psalm 119.165 NIV).

Paragraph Christianity

The first essay I assigned for my college freshmen composition class that I taught was the five-paragraph essay, but I would always clarify, "As you grow as writers, you will want to stop using this blueprint." The five-paragraph essay has all the components necessary to write an essay (thesis, facts, personal opinions, etc.), but it is a standard from which to experiment and creatively grow. Mature writers will take those same elements and produce something original and breathtaking.

I taught night classes, so I had a variety of students. However, I could somewhat organize them into groups. This grouping helped me to better serve my students' needs. First, I had my recent high school graduates. Some of these young students had the five-paragraph essay memorized. The others had heard of it, but they didn't understand all the elements and the purpose of it.

Next, I had returning students who hadn't touched a school book in years. If they had learned the basics of writing an essay, they didn't remember and had developed a fear of writing. Last, I had English as a Second Language (ESL) students. These students had acquired academic ideologies that were completely foreign to the western culture's style of expressing thought. Fundamental difficulties with language usage were hindrances for them, not to mention weaving words together to convey ideas.

Within all these groups, I had students who wanted to grow as writers and students who just wanted to pass and get as far away from writing as possible.

I say all this because I've been learning a lot about grace lately. I'm discovering that there is a five-paragraph Christianity (cultural Christianity) that is the basic standard of living out faith today. Five-paragraph Christianity definitely serves its purpose: it provides a blueprint with the basic elements of faith. The thesis of Christianity is that God is the Creator, Jesus is the Savior and the Holy Spirit is the Counselor, and we are called to love the Trinity and love others. The facts to support the thesis are found in the Bible. And the personal opinions come from the Holy Spirit's movement in our lives—our testimonies. But I have discovered that I have limited myself and others based upon a standard form of living our faith, and I have left no room for personal creativity and God's grace.

There are Christians who have grown up in Christian homes, knee-deep in Christian lifestyle. They know how to live by standard Christian expectations because they have seen it played out all of their lives. Some of them embrace the standard, finding security in the familiar; others, however, never understood the purpose of it and haven't found it fulfilling.

Moreover, there are Christians who have strayed from living out their faith. They haven't committed to any Christian disciplines (attending church, praying, reading the Bible, etc.) for many years, and they are scared about fitting in and/or learning to live by faith again. Finally, there are new Christians who know nothing about cultural Christianity. Praying is like talking to one's self, reading the Bible is like struggling through a boring history book and attending church is like going to the circus. Everything is strange and bewildering!

As a mentor, I would explain to all of them the importance of the Christian disciplines and try to illuminate the main thesis of Christianity. But I would also emphasize that Holy Spirit wants to mature us beyond the standard. I would point out that every influential leader in the Bible and church history was unique and part of a cutting-edge, Holy Spirit inspired movement. Christians who stand out grow beyond the norm of the day, reaching the changing people of tomorrow with the Gospel. I would tell them to cling closely to the Holy Spirit's guidance, and to use their God-given creativity to fulfill the amazing purposes that He has designed for them. Most importantly, I would urge them to put their hope and security in God and not people!

Many Christians (I included) have submitted to five-paragraph Christianity, and have not let themselves or others grow beyond the cultural standard. Because of fear or pride, we will not lean on God's grace and start creatively using the fundamental elements of Christianity to compose a beautiful, original essay that expresses the glory of God. The Body of Christ is made up of members, and we all have people that we directly impact. I for one want to encourage everyone in my sphere of influence to grow beyond the typical structure of cultural Christianity and live a life worth reading. Nevertheless, I want to be cognizant of the diversity of God's people and allow others the freedom to write their essays how they please.

I want to give grace to the Christian who is struggling with letting go of her comfort zone.

I want to give grace to the Christian who is still trying to come to terms with her faith.

I want to give grace to the Christian who has forsaken God but wants to recover her spiritual footing.

I want to give grace to the new Christian who finds everything about faith strange and confusing.

I will enlighten people to five-paragraph Christianity when they are just beginning or feeling lost, but I want to encourage Christians who are ready for growth to stretch beyond the norm into the unique direction God is calling them to. Whether they want to stick with the norm or take a step of faith into God's unknown is fine by me. I will love them either way. I will not judge nor will I compare; I choose to love and encourage.

There is so much freedom in allowing others to choose their own way. This freedom gives us more energy, creativity and grace to write our own essays for God. Let us by grace compose, side by side, our individual life stories so that the world can see the array of God's divine beauty poured out onto those who love Him.

"As God's co-workers we urge you not to receive God's grace in vain. For he says, 'In the time of my favor I heard you, and in the day of salvation I helped you'" (2 Corinthians 6.1-2 NIV).

Never a Writer

When I was fourteen years old, my family moved from Fairbanks, Alaska, to Corpus Christi, Texas. I was really excited. I would be starting high school in a beach town and I couldn't wait to get involved in the sports program! Playing sports was everything to me. I disciplined myself in sports, I enjoyed playing sports and much of my identity was wrapped up in sports. All I wanted was to move to Corpus Christi and start high school on the right foot – playing sports!

The sports I loved most were track, gymnastics, volleyball and softball. I played these sports from a young age, and I was confident that I would exceed in my new high school. When we moved to Corpus Christi, however, I discovered devastating news: the local high schools didn't have gymnastics, volleyball or softball—all they had was track! I couldn't believe it! Texas schools were about two things back then: cheerleading and football.

I floundered my first two years of high school. I never learned the discipline of studying or reading. I almost never did my homework, and I never read books. I would watch people read books, and I wondered what was going on in their minds. In fact, the first book I read all the way through was during our drive from Fairbanks to Corpus Christi. I devoured the book, and I couldn't believe all the beautiful images and emotions that went through my mind. I loved it! Yet, I still hadn't learned the discipline of reading, so I didn't pick up another book for several years.

During my freshmen year in high school, I felt hopeless and detached. I had lost my identity, my method of meeting friends (on the playing field) and my sense of achievement. Is it any wonder I accepted Jesus during this time? I struggled with feeling disconnected—I was in a new state, new culture, new climate (Corpus Christi never has a winter) and new changes in my body, and I had nothing to cling to for acceptance. I started studying a little bit more, and I was shocked when someone called me "the smart girl." Actually, I was thrilled! At least I had some kind of title!

During my sophomore year of high school, I ran track; but it wasn't the same. There was no sense of teamwork. I enjoyed my track friends, but I still didn't feel connected. Finally, my junior year in high school, I started tentatively writing. My grammar was pathetic, but I wrote with a lot of emotion. I felt a little tug toward writing, and I started writing in a journal (it is really embarrassing reading my high school journal and seeing just how desperately pitiful I was in high school).

My junior English teacher had us write an essay about Thomas Paine's famous line, "These are the times that try men's souls." We were supposed to research current social issues and discuss them in our essay. I, of course, didn't know how to research, so I wrote a satirical essay that made fun of the boys in our high school. I didn't realize that I was writing a satire, but I whipped up the essay (grammar mistakes and all) in about ten minutes.

The next week as I walked into class, my teacher had a big smile on her face and she told me how much she enjoyed my writing. She said that I should write for a magazine. She even read that essay to all of her classes.

I was ecstatic, and my waning self-esteem had a dramatic boost! I finally found something that I did well, and it had nothing to do with sports. My senior year, I took a creative writing class and I excelled. My grammar still wasn't great, but my teacher got excited about what I wrote. I started to get some confidence in my writing, and I began to integrate writing into my identity.

I went to college without any idea what degree plan I would take. I did, however, take a lot of English classes. I finally took a grammar class, and the hazy world of grammar started to become more clear. At the beginning of my junior year in college, my guidance counselor said that I would have to choose a degree plan. I was torn between majoring in Kinesiology or English. I finally chose English because I felt God pulling me in the direction of writing, which was strange because I wasn't much of a reader.

One day while I was in the mobile home that I shared with a friend in college, God told me that I was going to be a writer. I was twenty-one years old. I remember shrugging my shoulders and thinking to myself, "Well, I better start reading then." Once I knew that God wanted me to write, my writing improved dramatically. One English professor, whom I had taken for two semesters, even commented about the remarkable change in my writing. She contributed my writing improvement to her excellent teaching skills (she was a good teacher), but I never told her the full story. I finally had a God-given purpose, and I had a clear goal at which to aim.

I write all this because for years I never understood why God brought me clear across the country to a school that didn't have the sports that I loved. I always questioned God and wondered why my first two years of high school had to be so hard. It wasn't until a friend showed me her "life timeline" that I gained understanding.

My friend made a timeline of her life and wrote down the big events (bad and good) that happened to her. Then she looked at each event and asked the question, "Where was God's hand in this?" I discussed her timeline with her, and we were able to help her gain many beautiful insights of God's guidance in her walk of faith.

When I thought about my life, the first thing that came to my mind was my freshmen year in high school. It was very much a low point for me. However, I realized that if I had not gone through that struggle, I might not have become a Christian, and I definitely wouldn't be a writer. God in His awesome way allowed hardships in my life, so I could become who I am today. I can say with all honesty that I am glad I went through what I did. Of course, there is more to the story; but I'm glad God gave me clarity concerning this particular struggle. I look forward to the day that God gives me complete clarity about my life. I know I will be very glad that I trusted Him and stayed obedient to His will.

What about you? Do you want clarity about some of the events that happened in your life? Part of knowing God more intimately is knowing who you are in Christ. God says that you are a pleasing aroma to Him (2 Corinthians 2.15). You need to know the ingredients to that "aroma" so you can make that fragrance even more distinct for God. Moreover, the world needs to see who you are as a believer, and it is hard to be open about your Christianity when you have no clear identity as a believer.

I challenge each of you to make a timeline of your life. You can bring it before the Lord and ask Him to show you His hand in all the hard times and good times. I would also suggest you enlist a close friend to talk you through it, as well. I did this with my friend, and she came away with a better understanding of how God has moved in her life and how her circumstances have made her the sweet fragrance she is today.

Remember this: Your test becomes your testimony and your mess becomes your message. Strive to gain understanding about your walk of faith, and God will bless your efforts: "Blessed are those who find wisdom, those who gain understanding, for she is more profitable than silver and yields better returns than gold" (Proverbs 3.13-14 NIV).

God loves you, and He will match your heartache with His grace. Trust Him with your life. God is faithful, and He desires a strong relationship with you.

"God, who has called you into fellowship with his Son Jesus Christ our Lord, is faithful" (1 Corinthians 1.9 NIV).

The Book of Tomorrow

Tomorrow is a special day—I receive a box load of my newest book, *Our 6 His 7: Transformed by Sabbath Rest*, in the mail. What is so special about tomorrow is not so much the books themselves, but what I get to do with the books.

I wrote the book in 10 days from November 2 to November 12, 2014. My pastor's wife had asked me if I would speak to the interns at our church. These interns range from ages 18-25, and they serve the church for one year, receiving valuable ministry and corporate experience.

I prayed about speaking before I accepted. God has "sheltered" me from public ministry for many years, taking great care to build my personal ministry. When God freed me to talk to the interns, a floodgate of information came into my spirit. I began to write down everything the Holy Spirit wanted me to say, but it became apparent that there was a problem.

"God, there's no way I can share everything You are giving me in a 30-minute talk to the interns," I finally told Him.

"Write a book," God said simply.

"What?" I thought.

God knew that I was experiencing a barren season in my life that had caused great bitterness, which I was finally (by the power of the Holy Spirit) able to release. I had felt like all my writing was in vain, and I couldn't see any fruit from my years of effort. It was like my God-given dream had died.

When God asked me to write the book, I felt like Peter who had fished all night and caught nothing. And now Jesus was standing on the shore asking me to "Put out into deep water, and let down the nets for a catch" (Luke 5.4 NIV). This time I would agree to write a book, but I carried no expectations of my own—I did it simply out of obedience to the Lord.

Ten days later I was finished writing my first draft. I had pulled every fish (word) into my boat (book), and I was exhausted but joyous! It was a miracle! Less than a week later, I had the honor of telling this story to the interns.

I discussed the main elements of what God had revealed to me, and when the talk was over, they all said that they wanted a copy of my book. I didn't know what to tell them. I had no agent, no editor and no publisher for this book. I had merely written it by faith. I couldn't promise them something that I didn't know I could offer them, so I simply said, "I will try."

It's been about 3 months since I did that talk, and I was able to contact the director of the interns and let him know that I will be bringing the books by the church tomorrow. The interns are excited, and I am amazed at what God has done through my obedience.

I gave God my "yes" of faith, and He supernaturally provided in my life. Not only have I been blessed, but others will be blessed, as well. I'm glad I didn't carry any expectations with me while writing this book because God has done abundantly more than I could ever dream or imagine.

"Now to him who is able to do immeasurably more than all we ask or imagine, according to his power that is at work within us, to him be glory in the church and in Christ Jesus throughout all generations, for ever and ever! Amen" (Ephesians 3.20-21 NIV).

Start Somewhere

I struggled with writing my first novel, *Eve of Awakening.* God gave me the initial premise of the book when I was about 24 years old, but I didn't write it until I was 28. I had about 20 pages of the first draft completed when my pastor did a sermon series on Noah. He encouraged all the church members to change something about their life for 40 days that they knew God wanted them to change.

Some people quit doing something for 40 days—overeating, smoking, drug use, pornography, overspending, etc. Other people pledged to doing something for 40 days—exercising, saving money, reforming lost relationships, thinking positively, etc.

I committed to writing on my first novel for 40 days and wrote half the book. It would only take me a few months more to finish it. It was just after the new year almost in 2006 that I finished the first draft, and I so expected God to release publication possibilities right away. Nope.

It was funny. After I finished the book, I felt the Holy Spirit tell me to put it aside. I couldn't understand why because it was a miracle that I had even written it! Every time I tried to send my book to agents, I knew the Holy Spirit was telling me that my efforts would be fruitless.

God led me to a writers' conference several months later, and my book was denied by everyone. I wrote about an advanced society that seemed foreign to people, but years later with the changes in technology (smart phones, social media, Amazon, etc.), my book doesn't seem so far-fetched anymore.

The rejections I received were devastating, and I thought God had broken my heart. It would take many years for me to realize that it was my own expectations that broke my heart. God had promised to publish my book, but His timeline was never clear to me. I think if I would have known how long it would have taken and how much I would have to change, I would have admitted defeat before I ever began.

I finally set my book aside and began writing on my blog and serving in women's ministry leadership. God allowed ministry to transform me and then He called me out of it. I had three small children, and God wanted me to focus on the ministry of motherhood.

More years later, I rewrote my first draft of my book, and I felt the Holy Spirit leading me to enter my manuscript into a writing contest. No, I did not win, but winning wasn't the point. God wanted me to edit my book. Writing my book in the first place had been such a stretch for me that I told God that He would have to bring me someone to edit my book. Little did I know that God was shaping me into that editor.

I started editing three months before the contest deadline, and I became overwhelmed with how much work needed to be done. I thought I would be doing some simple changes, but instead I was rewriting the entire book. Finally, I only had 10 days left, and I was not even halfway done with the edits.

I'm not going make it, I told God. But He had no sympathy for me.

I opened my Bible and read, "If you have raced with men on foot and they have worn you out, how can you compete with horses? If you stumble in safe country, how will you manage in the thickets by the Jordan?" (Jeremiah 12.5 NIV).

"There's no way I can finish in time!" I yelled. God said nothing, waiting for what I would do.

I sat down at my laptop, bowed my head and prayed this prayer: "Holy Spirit, there is no way I can finish these edits on time without Your help. You will need to tell me exactly what to cut, what to change and what to add. I don't have time to wrestle through these edits. I need supernatural help."

And for 7 days the Holy Spirit was like a drill sergeant over my shoulder. Since I had three young children, I would write early in the morning, during nap time and late at night. I finally finished, and I whittled down my book from 125,000 words to 85,000 words. Although, it would take several more rewrites to complete the novel to what it is today, that time of editing was the most important.

After I had sent the novel off to the contest, I remember talking to God about how disappointed I was in my first draft. I was so impressed at the time I wrote it, but as I grew as a writer, I could see how much work my first draft needed. I wondered why God would have me write it at 28 when I obviously wasn't ready. I still needed much growth as a writer to be ready for publication.

God gave me an image of a person plowing a field for the first time. He plowed one field. Then he plowed another. Then he plowed several more fields until he finally came back to the initial field he had started with. He had to go back over his work on the first field because it wasn't plowed correctly.

With that image God said, "If that man hadn't plowed the first field, he would have never learned to plow the other fields. You must start in your weakness, so I can train you in My strength."

I realized that if I hadn't written the first draft in my incompetence, I would have never started the journey to writing well. You have to be bad at something before you can be good at it. We must all start somewhere, so we might as well start now!

Faith as a Second Language

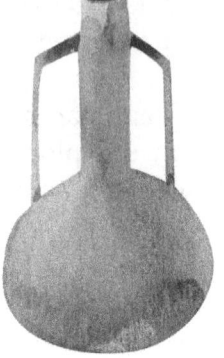

In graduate school, I was required to tutor a person learning English as a Second Language (ESL). I decided to talk with the local ESL teacher, and she allowed me to sit in a few of her classes. I befriended a beautiful woman from Vietnam. She and her husband owned a convenience store. Her husband spoke English fairly well because he ran the cash register and had to communicate with the customers. However, since she spent most of her time in the back of the store taking care of her home and family, her English was underdeveloped.

We met a few times before class and decided that I would start visiting her weekly at her convenience store. I eagerly wanted to help my new friend with her English, and I would try different methods of teaching her during each of our first sessions. Once, I brought a children's book with me and read it to her, but I could tell it didn't really make sense. Another time I brought the game, Scrabble, but that was too advanced. I tried several other activities, but none of them seemed to help her communicate better.

Finally, I found myself sitting with my friend face to face, listening to stories of her life and to the thoughts bubbling up in her heart. I was patient with her broken English and gave her loads of positive verbal and nonverbal cues. I allowed her plenty of time to collect her thoughts and express her feelings in a language so different from her own. As the weeks and months passed by, my friend's English improved and her confidence in communicating greatly increased. She felt comfortable talking with me, and her sense of security advanced her English language skills.

One of the stories my friend told me in her much-improved English made a deep impression on me. The story took place when she was pregnant with her twin boys four years earlier. She was new to America and she didn't know any English. She needed to make a doctor's appointment at the large city hospital, but she wound up weeping outside on one of the building's steps. She couldn't read any of the signs.

She couldn't speak with any of the employees. She didn't know where to go; and she felt lost, alienated and desperate for someone to understand and support her.

And I wonder if many new Christians feel like this. They begin a relationship with Christ and are suddenly plunged into this strange and amazing world of salvation.

They don't know the Christian lingo and they have trouble expressing their thoughts and feelings about faith. They may feel lost, alienated and desperate for someone to understand and support them. All they really need is someone to come alongside of them and help them find their footing in this new walk of faith.

I think the best thing we can do for new Christians is to sit with them—face to face—and listen to them with encouragement and reassurance. We can offer them the abundant grace and mercy that God has given us, so they can learn to feel comfortable and confident in their faith. Before all the studies, activities and expectations, we need to help them establish their security in Christ. And the best way to do this is to show them the same love Christ has shown us.

"So now I am giving you a new commandment: Love each other. Just as I have loved you, you should love each other. Your love for one another will prove to the world that you are my disciples" (John 13.34-35 NLT).

My Best Friend

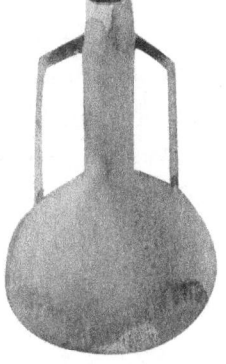

I've realized that when God is your best friend, you can't help but talk about Him. I remember when I struggled with talking about God and all the things He was showing me. I was uncomfortable, and I worried about what people would think. I had to push through my fears and literally force myself to pray in front of my kids, talk about the Bible to a friend or mention my faith to a stranger.

Apparently, something happened through the years. I went to a book club meeting the other night. The women had read my book, *Eve of Awakening*, and invited me to answer questions and discuss my writing journey. The club was not a Christian organization; though, there were quite a few Christians there. When I talked about my novel and the writing process, God was so thickly layered in all of my words. There was no skirting the issue of God, for my life revolved around Him.

Instead of inciting anxiety, my ease at discussing faith allowed the women to be liberal with their questions about all things God. They asked questions like "How do you hear God so easily?" and "Did you plan on God being a central theme of your book" and

"How do you talk to God?" I talked about the Holy Spirit's guidance in my life, and my reliance on the Lord was obvious to all of them.

The only thing I wish I would have explained better was the importance of Jesus. I have absolutely no ability to maintain a relationship with a holy God without the blood of Jesus. Because of the cross, my sins are washed away, and I have the righteousness of Christ covering me. It is only by the Pierced Lamb of God that I have access to a Holy God. Without Jesus, I wouldn't be able to enjoy the awesome relationship that I have with my Heavenly Father.

Luckily, most of the women in the group had a personal relationship with Jesus, and I know my words planted a seed in the other women's hearts. But next time I will be ready to talk about Jesus being the key to my entire walk of faith, which includes my journey as a writer.

"Jesus said to him, 'I am the way, the truth, and the life. No one comes to the Father except through Me'" (John 14.6 NKJV).

The Power of Editing

Most novice writers dive into writing their books, believing that when "The End" is written across the last line, their work is finished. Little do they know, however, that the art of crafting a novel has only just begun. Once the story leaves the writer's imagination and comes to life on the page, the intensely creative and exhaustive work of editing takes center stage.

I wrote my debut novel, *Eve of Awakening*, in about four months, but it would take years of editing and rewriting to make my story print worthy. Even after my eyes had traveled along hundreds of pages and thousands of lines from start to finish over and over again, other eyes were still necessary to find things that I had missed. And the more eyes, the better.

Editing causes an overweight and out of shape manuscript to become toned, developed and attractive. Editing chisels away the unnecessary glut, beautifies the mundane, thickens the emotional stimuli and brings the "wow-factor" into the ordinary. At a release party, editing can transform a book from an ignored wallflower to a debutante that everyone wants to meet.

I personally look at the first draft of the manuscript to *Eve of Awakening* and thank God that it never made it into the hands of prospective publishers. Through the years, I cut the wordcount dramatically, rewrote the last two chapters and revolutionized the dialogue. Though the heart of my story remains; the readability, appeal and impact of my novel is better able to leave a lasting impression on my readers—all by the power of editing!

So don't see editing as a chore. See it as an opportunity to awaken your story's best self! Take time and care while you edit, allow others to offer constructive criticism and unleash the awe-inspiring masterpiece hidden just beneath the layers of drafts. A novel that changes lives is ready to be born; you simply need to nurture its development for a season until the story is empowered to soar.

"But you, take courage! Do not let your hands be weak, for your work shall be rewarded" (2 Chronicles 15.7 ESV).

God wants to edit our lives, as well. We are a beautiful masterpiece in His hands, and He will edit our lives to its best version possible if we let Him. He sees the beginning from the end, and He knows what to edit, add and change in our story.

"I make known the end from the beginning, from ancient times, what is still to come. I say, 'My purpose will stand, and I will do all that I please'" (Isaiah 46.10 NIV).

God wants our lives to impact the world around us, so He'll involve Himself in every detail, tweaking our story line by line. He is the Perfect Editor, and we can trust that He will produce the greatness He desires in our lives.

"Trust in the Lord with all your heart; do not depend on your own understanding. Seek his will in all you do, and he will show you which path to take" (Proverbs 3.5-6 NLT).

The Neo-Anchorites

The medieval anchorites secluded themselves in anchorholds, which were usually small cells built into the sides of churches. These anchorites would devote themselves to prayer, fasting and reading the Bible. Since they were freed from many of the distractions of the outside world, they had frequent opportunities to seek God. Many people would drop by the anchorholds, so they could discuss spiritual matters with the anchorites. The anchorites could offer a truth-centered opinion that gave their listeners a better understanding of the Holy Spirit's movement in their lives.

Though times and culture have changed, modern day anchorites are beginning to rise up everywhere. They are making themselves comfortable in anchorholds all over the Internet. They write from their little "cells" and share what the Holy Spirit is teaching them. They frequently pull from the outside world in order to devote hours communing and writing with God each week. They seek God's heart, movement and will and post all the revelations the Holy Spirit is giving them; so others can find encouragement, strength and understanding.

The neo-anchorites are called "Christian Bloggers," and I would like to applaud them today.

I know you spend hours each week seeking God and many more hours writing.

I know that God has sifted your life, making more room for Him.

I know you selflessly write each post without concern of money or recognition.

I know God has humbled you, so you can rely whole-heartily on Him.

I know at times you question your sacrifice.

I know how just one inspired reader fills you with joy.

I know the pressure of an un-written revelation, waiting to be shared.

I know that your efforts are many times trivialized.

I know you have given up much of your personal time to blog.

But I want to encourage that everything birthed out of the Spirit has eternal ramifications. You might not get a degree, a paycheck or a contract; but God is bringing people to your doorstep, and they are finding nourishment from your words. Blogging can be a humbling, lonely ministry; but God is using your free-will offerings to establish His glory and further His kingdom. You are reaching people for Christ in a new frontier, and you will light a path in the darkness.

"Let us not become weary in doing good, for at the proper time we will reap a harvest if we do not give up" (Galatians 6.9 NIV).

Bushy Eyebrows

While my husband drove us home from church, I sat irritated in the passenger seat. The sermon was amazing—all about expecting "greatness" from God. This reminder used to encourage me; but after years of waiting for God to publish my first book, I felt disillusioned.

I've been down this road many times—trekking down the Valley of Baca going from spring to spring on my journey to meet God in Zion (Psalm 84). I didn't want God to refresh my soul again because I knew it meant another year of trekking, another year of sacrificing my nights sowing my words without a harvest, another year of believing God's promises by His faithfulness alone. Another year…

He promised me when I was young and ignorant that I would write books for Him, but I never realized how difficult and long the journey would be. I never thought that I would beg Him to take the desire away, so I could walk away from it all. How would it feel to live free from the destiny-burden He created for me?

As I huffed in my chair, I thought of all the dreams I had given up to follow God's bidding. Maybe I could dabble a little bit in my old dreams. I could teach a college class or two. I could write a few articles for the newspaper. I could shut out the voice of the Holy Spirit always telling me what to say and write. I could…

I flipped down the mirror on the visor and analyzed my face. Who was I and what was I doing? As I stared at myself, I noticed a stray hair on my eyebrow that I forgot to pluck. Instantly, I came out of my introspection and grabbed my purse to find tweezers.

As I looked, I felt the Holy Spirit say, "You teaching a college class is like that stray hair. It doesn't fit the shape of your design."

God has an exciting and unique plan for each of us, and we must carefully groom our steps to fit His purpose. There are many wonderful achievements we can pursue, but if they are not a part of God's will for us, they become idols. The worst decision we can make is to cheat on God's best for our lives with seemingly good things. We need to pluck out everything that doesn't align with God's plan, so that our purpose is plainly visible and distinct.

We don't want undefined lives….or bushy eyebrows.

"He cuts off every branch of mine that doesn't produce fruit, and he prunes the branches that do bear fruit so they will produce even more" (John 15.2 NLT).

Striving Laundry

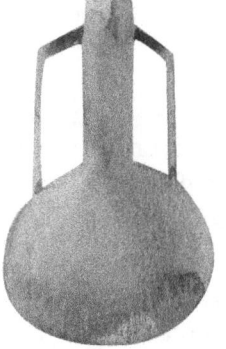

I have been anxiously striving to finish edits on my first book. My mind has been consumed with writing, and I'm constantly telling myself to get to work. I feel the pressure of a deadline, and I told God one afternoon, "I can't wait until I'm done."

I could sense God smile and say, "Then you'll start your second book."

I stopped in my tracks. I realized that I will never be finished. When I'm done climbing this mountain, God will have another one for me in the distance. While I'm alive on this earth, God will always place promises for my life in the horizon.

God places promises beyond each of us; and as we move closer to them, God is able to mold us into the likeness of His Son. Promises are in the core of Jesus; they pull us toward Him like gravity and slowly perfect us into our best design.

At that moment, I had a reality check. Obviously, my perspective was wrong because God would not want me to be anxious about anything (Philippians 4.6).

How do we strive towards God's promises without becoming overwhelmed? How do we find balance and joy in a life that will always be pulled toward higher goals and greater accomplishments? I would like to answer this profound question with one simple word: Laundry.

Laundry is never done. Whenever I go from room to room with arms filled with dirty clothes, I like to sing the theme song to the 1984 movie, *The Never Ending Story*.

I've learned to do a little bit of laundry every day. I don't even think about it anymore. When I wake up, I'll notice that the hamper is getting full, so I'll grab the clothes and start a load. That afternoon after I put the kids down for a nap, I'll put the clothes into the dryer and forget about them. While the kids are playing before bed, I'll take the load out, fold it and put it away. Never once was I anxious.

I used to let the laundry build up, but I noticed that I always became anxious. The lack of clean clothes would begin to affect my life, and my mind would send me distracting signals to "get to work." Laundry would become a big deal, when, in reality, it is such a small part of my life. If I would simply give laundry a fraction of my attention every day, it would be manageable.

This concept is the same for God's promises. God doesn't want His promises to become anxiety builders in our lives. His promises are supposed to draw us closer in relationship with Him. The imbalance comes when we stop daily focusing on God, and we let our lack of time with Him build up, unused in the hamper.

If we hungrily seek God every day and align our lives with His will, He will ensure that we have just enough time every day to work on His promises. As we seek God, He will prune our lives of everything unnecessary, and we will have the perfect amount of time to complete His will each day. Also, when we focus on God, He will fill us with joy and peace that will filter through every aspect of our lives, dispersing our anxiety, worry and procrastination.

The purpose of life is to glorify God. If we are not doing that in our daily life, we probably need to ask God for a healthy dose of perspective. I decided to give up on striving; instead, I'm keeping my eyes on God and allowing His grace to move me toward His best for my life.

"Cease striving and know that I am God; I will be exalted among the nations, I will be exalted in the earth" (Psalm 46.10 NASB).

A Writer's Weakness

"Don't judge a weakness that someone has," I always tell my kids. "Because that weakness is linked to a strength that you don't have."

I am a writer, which means I am an introvert, I overthink and I struggle with negative thoughts. I know not all writers are introverts, especially now that a million books were self-published in 2017. Over 80% percent of people say they want to write a book and with the advent of on-demand publishing, anyone can. I'm an indie writer, and I definitely believe it's an awesome way to publish.

Yet, not everyone has the design, calling and passion to create stories and relay information without thought to fame, money and recognition. A true writer MUST write. It is not a stream of income. It is not a hobby. It is not a check on a bucket list. It is an integral part of who he or she is, and to avoid it would be a travesty leading to a slow death of heart and soul.

For me, the need to write became like a fire in my chest (Jeremiah 20.9), burning until finally at age 28, I began writing my first novel, *Eve of Awakening*. With every book completed, I had to create yet another one. Almost 15 years and over 20 books later, I still feel that burning, but it is spreading to editing, publishing and teaching.

"Publish his glorious deeds among the nations. Tell everyone about the amazing things he does" (Psalm 96.3 NLT).

With this passion to write comes a bombardment of self-awareness, inwardness and rumination. Yes, these are strengths that help me to write fiction and non-fiction with emotion, appeal and tension. However, these strengths are linked to the deep-seated weaknesses of over-analyzing, negative self-talk, intense criticism and self-doubt.

In my early thirties, God gave me a Psalm of King David to help me with my struggle. I wrote it on my hand every day for a season.

"...Your gentleness has made me great" (Psalm 18.35 NKJV).

I needed to learn gentleness, self-compassion and grace. I love the strengths found in my introvertedness. I love creating scenes and watching my characters come to life. I love sitting alone at the keyboard and considering life, faith and purpose and expressing how I feel. But I hate the sinister underbelly of those strengths that ooze out into my soul and try to stink up my life.

Satan knows my weaknesses. He looked me over, summed me up and beat me down. He knew exactly when and where to attack—every morning in my mind. Satan knows my weaknesses are linked to strengths that he hates, proclaiming the goodness of God and salvation through Christ. He seethes over it, so better attack me before my eyes open.

However, he didn't realize that the more he attacked, the more I fought back. My mornings and days became a warring ground of proving that I was a good writer, that I was worthy in Christ and that I had a purpose despite my imperfections.

But fighting can only last so long. Sooner or later our strength wanes, and we wonder why everything has to be so polarized.

I just finished writing the first draft of my Bible study, *Why Jesus: a 50 Day Holy Spirit Experience,* and I have been rescued. I needed a deeper sense of all that salvation entails: Jesus loves me, He died to take my place, He has given me His victory and He has taken the dark underbelly of all my weaknesses and now His power is made perfect in them.

The negative pathways that my brain has dug from years of fighting the enemy's attacks have become a powerful highway for Christ's power to flow. In all those areas of struggle, Christ is standing tall, resolute and awe-inspiring. I'm reminded of a verse from Shakespeare's play, *Julius Caesar.*

"Why, man, he doth bestride the narrow world
Like a Colossus, and we petty men
Walk under his huge legs and peep about
To find ourselves dishonorable graves."

Except in my version of this verse, Jesus is bestriding the pathways of my mind that Satan has forged. And the enemy of my soul peeps about Christ's huge legs, knowing that the victory has been won and he's the sore loser with the dishonorable grave.

So now I can boast about my weaknesses, knowing Christ is standing strong in them. And I can't help but laugh because what the enemy meant for my destruction has backfired in his face (Genesis 50.20). His attacks caused me to run to the throne of God and lean into the grace of Jesus.

"But he said to me, 'My grace is sufficient for you, for my power is made perfect in weakness.' Therefore I will boast all the more gladly about my weaknesses, so that Christ's power may rest on me" (2 Corinthians 12.9 NIV).

Formatting Life

There are many aspects to writing books. One of the final stages—besides publishing and marketing—is formatting the book. This can be one of the most tedious, laborious, frustrating and time-consuming aspects of writing. Trying to transfer a huge word document into publishing software creates havoc on almost every page of the book.

Also, books in our current generation can't just be words on a page. There needs to be pretty, little details at the start of the book and the beginning of every chapter. Some books even add details to every page! Having to add these details is also very tedious work. You have to really know your word processor in order to fully use the tools available to you. And once you figure out the best way to format your book, you have to go through each page many times over until everything is perfect.

On one particular day, I was formatting a collection of devotionals. I was adding details to the beginning of each chapter, and the process seemed slow and boring. However, after a few clicks, I felt like I was getting into a groove. It was almost like the word processor was reading my thoughts and was anticipating what I needed. But I knew that wasn't the case. The word processor is unchanging. It was I who had finally adapted myself to the word processor, which created a beautiful, consistent flow to the formatting process.

The same goes for our lives of faith. God is perfect and unchanging. Though His movements morph to each generation, person and situation, He Himself is always perfect and holy. The struggle we face begins when we try to adjust our lives to Him. Our imperfection collides with His perfection, and we go through growing pains—a shaping of our character into the image of Jesus.

We finally feel a smooth flow in our lives, not when He has changed, but, rather, when we have changed, submitting to His will and standard. The struggle is real and difficult, and we may want to give up; but if we keep working at it, we will find a flow in our unity with God. When this happens, God is able to do so much more in our lives than we ever thought possible. We just need to get into His groove and hang on for the wild ride!

"For I the Lord do not change…" (Malachi 3:6 ESV).

I pray you enjoyed this collection of meditations. I would be honored if you would write a review on Amazon. You can find my other fiction and non-fiction books at Amazon or on my blog, www.alisahopewagner.com.